Walt F.J. Goodridge, author of *Turn Your Passion Into Profit,* presents:
The Turn Your Passion Into Profit™ "Quick Start" Manual (2014/2015)

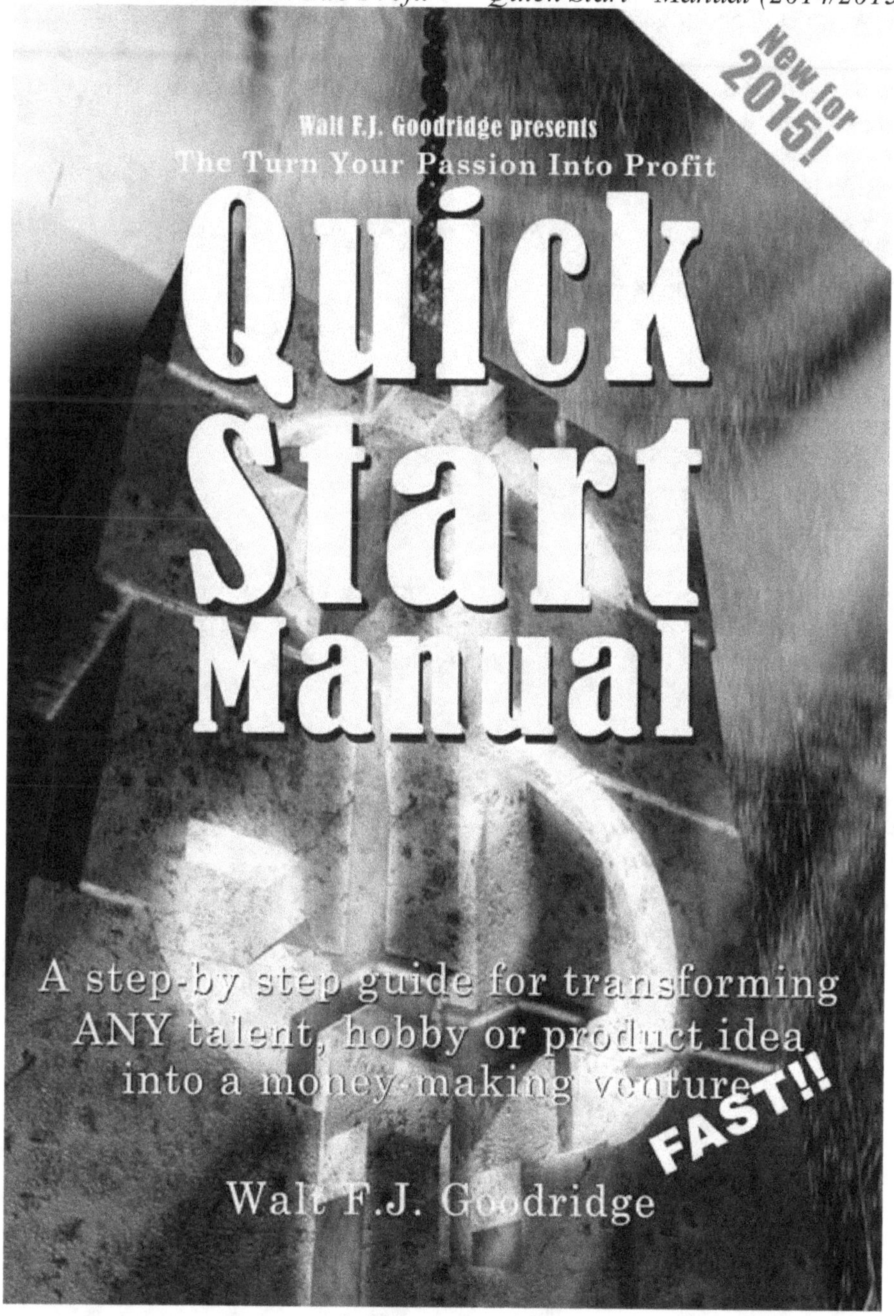

Walt F.J. Goodridge presents
The Turn Your Passion Into Profit

New for 2015!

Quick Start Manual

A step-by-step guide for transforming
ANY talent, hobby or product idea
into a money-making venture

FAST!!

Walt F.J. Goodridge

A 100-step guide
for getting your passion-centered business up and running…FAST!
A supplement to *Turn Your Passion Into Profit™*
the original passion-to-profit guidebook first published in 1999
(and updated just about every year since)

Published by The Passion Profit Company, an imprint of
a company called W, New York

The Passion Profit Company
P.O. Box 618
Church Street Station
New York, NY 10008-0618

Distributed exclusively by
A company called W doing business as
The Passion Profit Company
www.PassionProfit.com
orderdept@passionprofit.com
phone: (646) 481-4238

Retail Cost: $19.95
ISBN-10: 1451545703
ISBN-13: 9781451545708

Printed in the United States of America

Dedication
This book is Dedicated to Isolene Rebecca Golding
Before, 1907-1988, and beyond

Photo Credits:
Cover image, "Forging A Fortune" by Colin Anderson

TABLE OF CONTENTS

The Founder's Mission

"I am proud to offer the world a philosophy and formula for turning one's passion into profit. I encourage its use by parents, teachers, coaches, as well as within institutions of higher learning. It is my hope that this information will foster a greater understanding and appreciation of our inherent value as spiritual beings and the expression of that value within the physical marketplace. It is my wish that these ideas lead a revolution in thought and indeed and usher in a new era of entrepreneurial expression, financial independence, and personal freedom."

— Walt F.J. Goodridge
aka: The Passion Prophet, Founder of the PassionProfit Movement

The PassionProfit™ Philosophy

Your PASSION is part of your life's purpose
EVERYONE has a passion
ALL passions have value
ANY passion can be turned into profit

The PassionProfit™ Formula: The Cycle of Success

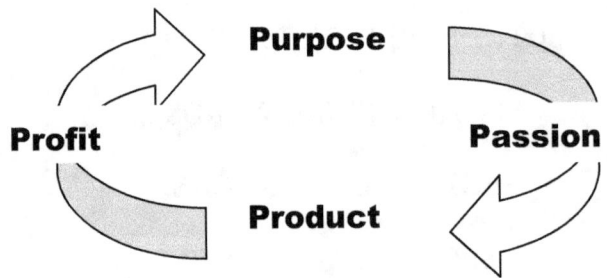

The Promise: Value No One Can Steal

"If you create and market a product or service through a business that is in alignment with your personality, capitalizes on your history, incorporates your experiences, harnesses your talents, optimizes your strengths, complements your weaknesses, honors your life's purpose, and moves you towards the conquest of your own fears, there is ABSOLUTELY NO WAY that anyone in this or any other universe can offer the same value that you do!"

SECTION: ORIENTATION

"Document the journey for future reference!"

1. ❑ Complete the course sign-in & registration ❑

My name is: _____

My domain name(s): _____

My Passionpreneur identity ("What do I do?"): _____

My Product or service: _____

Date Quick Started: _____ Date Launched: _____

Date of first sale: _____

Important note: The information concerning business structures, business addresses, licenses, etc., are based on United States standards.

2. ❏ Understand the goal of this manual ❏

"The only way to take control of your life, raise your standard of living and move beyond merely surviving is to create your own unique product or service that you offer to increasing numbers of people in exchange for the things of value that you desire. This simple formula applies to countries as well as people. A self-sufficient economy has its own products or services of value to export to the world. Similarly, a self-sufficient individual has something of value to exchange in the global marketplace. That thing of value is based on your natural talent, skill, or interest—in other words, your passion!"--Walt F.J. Goodridge, author of *Turn Your Passion Into Profit*™

My goal to help you achieve that control of your life. The goal of this manual is to empower you with specific tools and techniques you can use to bring the things of value you possess (your talent and passion) to the marketplace successfully, profitably and quickly!

3. ❏ Commit to using this manual effectively ❏

In this manual, I'm going to share with you the essential steps to get up and running—tips and techniques I've used to launch my own as well as my clients' businesses. Many of the tasks need to be implemented pretty much simultaneously. Other tasks are ongoing, and need to be revisited at various points on your journey. However, I've arranged them all in as close to a sequential order as possible. Here are a few tips to get the most benefit:

(a) To get the most from this manual, never continue reading past a word or phrase you don't understand! It's been shown that the only reason people give up on a new project or course of study is that they encounter a word, phrase or concept for which they have no definition, or the wrong definition. If a word in this guide is new to you, please use the glossary, dictionary or the Internet to find the most appropriate meaning. This tip is more important than most people know!

(b) Use the checkboxes! (❏) After you've read and performed the necessary activity, or are sure you understand its significance, place a check in the box, initial it, place the date next to it, then proceed. Think of this manual as an agreement between your present self and your future self. Your initials represent signing an agreement to live true to your evolving self, your dreams, and goals.

(c) Read this guide at least twice! I encourage you to read the guide once for a general overview, and then again to take notes and action! There's also a second set of checkboxes for your future reading and implementation.

(d) DO NOT skip around or perform the steps in some other order. EXCEPTION: Even though I suggested you proceed in the order I've laid out in this manual, one of the greatest abilities you'll need to master is how to separate unconnected events in order to move forward. I'll give you a simple example:

Most people believe they have to actually write a book before they can sell it. It seems like a logical progression, doesn't it? However, I've learned that those two events—the completion and the selling—are actually unconnected. I can and do, in fact, pre-sell my books, and start collecting money months *before* the book actually exists—sometimes even before I've written a single word!

Business is full of opportunities like this to move forward in non-traditional, counter-intuitive ways; ways that allow you to get from point "A" to point "D" and filling in points "B" and "C" later on!

Tip: As you move forward, look ahead to the next step and ask yourself "Can I take this next step NOW?" "Do I really need to wait for step 5 to be complete before step 6?" Get in the habit of pushing yourself forward in this way.

(e) Work from a daily task list! Make morning list of all the day's tasks!

(f) Email your questions! (walt@passionprofit.com. I will personally answer so you get the most value from this manual, and it helps improve future editions for other passionpreneurs.

4. ❏ Meet the pre-requisites ❏

This manual is designed to help you get started as quickly as possible with the launch of your new passion-centered business. It was created specifically for those who have been exposed to the Passion Profit™ Philosophy and Formula. Therefore, I suggest you

(a) Read *Turn Your Passion Into Profit* or listen to the audio edition

(b) Take the Passionpreneur Personality Test http://www.passionprofit.com/itest

(c) Read *Websites That Sell* after reading this manual

For the purpose of this manual, I'm going to assume that (a) your product is a viable and sellable book, cd, video, subscription or some other product, (b) that it can be manufactured and delivered relatively inexpensively through regular channels (i.e. postal delivery), and/or (c) that can be emailed, downloaded or accessed online, or (b) that it may be a service you can offer online or by phone (translation, consulting, etc.) Now, even if your product or service does NOT meet these assumptions perfectly, 90% of this information in this manual will still be valuable and applicable.

5. ❑ Intro: Consider this scenario ❑

Let's pretend I am your business coach and advisor, and you've come to me with an idea for a product or service you want to sell, and to launch a passion-centered business around it as quickly as possible. I say:

"It does NOT take years, months, weeks, or even days to start a business and start making money. We can do it in hours, or even minutes, make our first sale just as quickly, and I'm going to show you how. Let's get started!"—Walt

Would you believe me? Well, the fact is: even though this is a practical, how-to guide with actions designed to achieve a specific outcome, the key to your success in this or any endeavor is not solely a function of action, but one of belief. In other words the people who will succeed at launching a passion-centered business quickly and turn their passions into profit, are the people who embark on this journey with the ardent *belief* and conviction that it is possible to do so.

If you do not *really* believe a goal is possible for you, you can implement all the action steps in the world, and *still* not be successful. Why? Well, it works like this: your belief level affects the thoughts you think. Your thoughts influence your confidence, your courage and even your creativity. Your creativity determines the types of ideas you come up with, the colors you choose for your site and logo, the words you use in your headlines and sales copy, and a whole set of specifics and intangibles that will affect your success. In other words, people who "believe" they will succeed act more confidently, take more risks, create more dynamic products, and use different words and ideas and images to communicate than people who don't believe. It makes sense, doesn't it? Therefore, anything you can do to raise your belief level will help improve the quality of your product, your sales copy, your website, and thus the overall impact of your business.

To raise your belief level, I suggest you read about other successes, seek out and speak with people who are doing what you wish to do, take self-help courses, read, listen to or watch informational and inspirational books, videos and audio programs, and immerse yourself in the world of entrepreneurial success.

The ideal scenario is to find someone who's already doing what you wish to do and who can coach you. Now, I'd love to be able to coach everyone, but since, practically speaking, I can't, this manual will serve as a way for me to be your virtual coach to help you through the process of turning your passion into profit.....FAST! Let's get started!

6. ❑ Read more testimonials to raise your belief level ❑

To help raise your belief level, read some of the many PassionProfit™ testimonials at http://www.passionprofit.com/testimonials

7. ❏ Get on the same page ❏

In the appendix of *Turn Your Passion into Profit*, there is a comprehensive list of books for your suggested reading. However, in the interest of a quick start, these are five I suggest you read *before* we work together:

The E-Myth Revisited: Why Most Small Businesses Don't Work and What to Do About It by Michael E. Gerber

A few years ago, Entrepreneur® Magazine asked me to write an article for which I interviewed several million-dollar passionpreneurs and asked them the secret to success. Almost every single one of them credited what they learned in this book to helping them think differently about business in general and about their own businesses in particular, and made the single most significant impact in the results they achieved.

The 22 Immutable Laws of Branding by Al and Laura Ries

This is an amazing book I refer to again and again each time I launch a new idea. The principles they present and explain—along with real world examples—are vital keys to creating winning brands for your products and services.

No B.S. Marketing to the Affluent by Dan Kennedy

It seems almost laughably obvious, but the best way to "recession-proof" your business is to raise your prices and sell to the people with money—those who are affected least and last by recession. You should also REFUSE to compete with others on price, but to present yourself based on uniqueness and value in order to justify your prices. Dan Kennedy shows you how.

The Science of Getting Rich by Wallace Wattles

This book is now in the public domain, so there are free copies widely available throughout the internet. There's even an audio version you can download free of charge at archive.org. We've got our own specially-edited PassionProfit™ version available at www.passionprofit.com/resources/sogr. You can never get enough of these classic thoughts!

Secrets of the Millionaire Mind by T. Harv Eker

I can show you how to *generate* money, but unless you know how to *attract and keep* it, it will flow through your hands like air. Trust me, I know this from personal experience. Understanding what T. Harv Eker calls your "money blueprint" is perhaps the single most important part of turning your passion sustainably into profit.

Do not underestimate the importance of any of information in these books.

8. ❑ Understand the idea of a "quick start" ❑

Now, I define a Passion to Profit "Quick Start" as *"going from passion idea to income (i.e. your first sale) in the shortest time possible."* In order to "quick start" your passion-centered business, you will need a few things in place:
1. a basic business structure
2. a potential product/service
3. a way to communicate its value to the world
4. a way to exchange value (i.e. accept money)

To communicate your product's (or service's) value to the world, you'll need:
a. a list of potential customers and/or "gatekeepers"
b. a website that sells
c. a marketing/public relations strategy

To exchange value and accept money, you'll need:
b. a bank account
c. merchant status
a. an online "shopping cart" or other payment system (fax/mail order/COD)

9. ❑ Focus on completion rather than perfection ❑

In quick start mode, our goal is *"completion, rather than perfection."* In other words, we want to get things done This does not mean we will be doing shoddy work or offering substandard products. It simply means that our primary focus will be to get up and running knowing we can always fix any mistakes and correct any errors as we proceed. In order to develop the mindset necessary for this way of doing business, read how to separate unconnected events next.

10. ❑ Practice how to separate unconnected events ❑

In my book, *Living True To Your Self,* I explain that one of the key skills to develop in order to make your life proceed the way you want it to, is the ability to separate unconnected events. In project management, they call it finding the critical path—*"the sequence of activities that must be completed on schedule for the entire project to be completed on schedule."* Some activities/events are on the critical path to reaching your goal, while others are not. Let me explain how that might apply to quick-starting your business.

When completing a project or achieving any goal in life, many people are trained to think sequentially, or in linear terms. In other words, they perform task "A" then task "B," then task "C" believing that the tasks must be performed in that order. In their minds the events are connected by a single line (hence the term linear). However, that assumption may not be entirely true.

Let's suppose you are in the process of being approved for your Paypal™ Website Payments Pro account, and therefore, have not yet finalized your merchant status to be able to accept credit cards, but someone calls you today to place a credit card order. What would you do? Many people would tell the potential customer some version of *"Sorry, we can't accept credit cards right now. Can you send a check?"* End result: you lose an immediate sale.

I, on the other hand, would handle it a little differently. I would thank the customer, gladly take the order, the credit card information, expiration date, address, CVV number, billing address and shipping address, and promptly fill the customer's order. (I might, however, tell the customer that the order will ship in a few days, giving myself enough time for my merchant application to be approved, at which time I would charge the customer's card, and ship their order.) I might even take the chance and actually ship the order out and hope that the customer's card is valid when I eventually charge it at some point in the future. Result: I make an immediate sale!

You don't need to have the merchant account in place in order to take credit card orders. For that matter, you don't need to have anything at all in place in order to take orders. Separate selling a book from actually have a book to sell. Separate accepting credit card orders from actually having the means to charge the card. The events are not connected by a single line in a fixed order and sequence, they are not in series, they are in parallel (side by side). You can do one even if the other isn't in place.

In fact, I'll go a step further and say you don't even need to have a product before you start making money selling it! In 1994, customers who bought my first book about starting a record label, started contacting me to write a similar book about starting an artist management company. I took their advice, and when I decided to write that second book, I sent out letters along with an order form asking those same customers to send their money now to "pre-order," and that I would fill their orders in 2-3 months when the book was complete. And guess what? They did just that! As a result, I was able to finance the production of my second book with money from my customers who purchased on faith, based on my reputation and my promise to do what I said I would!

Experiences like that helped me understand that certain events I *thought* were connected weren't really connected at all in reality, but merely in my mind, and that if I could separate them in my mind, I could accomplish much more, move forward quickly, create momentum, and achieve the results I desired.

Admittedly, this sort of strategy requires a certain tolerance for risk and uncertainty, and this sometimes causes people to worry:
What if I don't get approved for my merchant account?
Answer: Take the loss, or simply contact the customer and ask for a different form of payment.

What if I don't finish the book when I said I would?
Answer: Send the pre-paid customers an apology letter and offer them some sort of bonus for their patience. Refund anyone who gets nasty.

In other words, as long as you have a "plan b" and are comfortable with any scenario that plays out (and no scenario is life threatening, you know, it's all small stuff), you, and your reputation will survive.

Practicing the art of separating unconnected events also requires that you be confident about being able to fulfill your promises and honor your commitments, complete an action and get things done in a timely manner. It requires that you have a clear vision of where you're heading and know that you will get there, BUT, that if for some reason things don't work out the way you anticipate, that it's not the end of the world. The consequences are rarely fatal.

As you proceed to Quick Start your business, ask: "Do I really need to do "A" before "B?" Can I do "C" (my actual goal) first, and then come back later and do "A?"" You'd be surprised just how creative and successful you can become (don't break any laws) separating unconnected events!

11. ❑ Envision a preliminary brand identity ❑

The next thing we need to do is get an initial idea of how we will present your product or service to the market. What will the title/name be? How can we make a catchy title/name to sell it? Does the concept lend itself to creating follow-up products and services? We want to make sure this trade name or brand is sellable both online and off. Is there a catchy and memorable domain name we can use to sell it? In other words, we want to start envisioning the brand identity.

This initial product and branding brainstorming is necessary at this point because it may impact some of the details of how we set up the business.

SECTION: BASIC BUSINESS STRUCTURE

Perform these tasks immediately!

Important note: The information concerning business structures, business addresses, licenses, etc., are based on United States standards.

12. ❑ Choose an INITIAL business structure ❑

Many new entrepreneurs often get stuck at this very first step. They can't decide whether to start a sole proprietorship, corporation, LLC, etc., and never move beyond. Remember, we're in quick start mode here. We're focused on completion rather than perfection. You always have the freedom to start accepting money for your value at any time, and then formalizing the actual structure at a later date. Therefore, I suggest you consider your business an individual sole proprietorship initially (you can use your social security number or apply for a tax ID number using IRS form SS-4*), and then, you can always "upgrade" to a more formal business structure later. *(*Applies to US residents)*

13. ❑ Get a business address in your country of choice ❑

At least here in the United States, you can do business using a post office box address. You do not need to rent actual office space.

14. ❑ Do you have a bank account? ❑

Your bank account can be personal checking or savings account for now. For quick start purposes, it doesn't have to be in the name of the business at this time. You can use a personal bank account and then change to a business account later. Your bank account doesn't even have to be with a physical bank! You could set up an online-only account as long as they have a routing number (ABA number) (eg. home.capitalone360.com, formerly ING Direct)

15. ❑ Do you have a Paypal account? ❑

WHY: You'll need a way to accept money from your customers. Paypal is not your only option for online sales, of course, but a great majority of US-based folks who may be your potential customers have Paypal accounts and you want to make it easier for them to do business with you.

Paypal and their "Website Payments Pro" option are great because:
- money from sales is immediately deposited into your Paypal™ account
- their Paypal™ debit card gives you immediate access to your funds
- you won't need a "payment gateway" to process credit card orders
- you won't need separate merchant approval from Visa/MC, Discover or Amex
- the per-transaction fee Paypal charges is comparable to other options
- Paypal is typically more lenient approving people with poor credit (like me!)

16. ❑ Get a personal or business credit/debit card ❑

You'll need this in order to make purchases and pay for certain products and services for your business. If you're not into having credit or debit cards in your name linked to bank accounts, you can purchase a prepaid debit card at certain convenience stores.

17. ❑ Set up voicemail ❑

You can set up a free Google Voice account to accept phone calls. Visit http://google.com/voice for more details

18. ❑ Set up fax line or fax service to receive orders ❑

If you don't have a dedicated fax line in your home or place of business, you can use an online fax service like efax, myfax, etc. I would advise against using the same line you use for voice calls for your incoming faxes. It's quite annoying to your potential customers to call for one only to get the other!

19. ❑ Prepare to accept credit card payments ❑

Paypal™ is also a credit card (visa/mc/discover/amex) merchant processor. Therefore, if you're not personally able to qualify as a merchant (due to bad credit history), Paypal may be a good option for you.

20. ❑ Prepare to accept phone orders ❑

Get a separate Google -Voice number and forward it to your cell phone or land line. You can use that number strictly for direct over-the-phone orders.

Get a separate Google Voice number and set up the voicemail feature to use it for general incoming customer service calls and inquiries.

Paypal's business account comes with a "virtual terminal" feature, so you won't even need a physical terminal (card swiping machine) to charge your customers. Simply log in to your Paypal account and enter the customer's credit card information into the secure form for real time processing.

Go to Paypal.com, sign up for a "Business" account (or choose "Premier" account and upgrade later.)

21. ❑ Get an email account for doing business ❑

Even if you don't have a *joeandmary@mycompany.com* email account yet, you can set up *mycompany@gmail.com* so you can quick start!

22. ❑ Perform these tasks later ❑

Remember, for quick start success, focus on completion, not perfection. The following can be completed, changed, upgraded, tweaked or modified later.

☐ *Get a tax id number*

This will vary depending on your country, but in the US, you can use your social security number to do business as an individual. You can always change the structure of your business later.

☐ *Decide on your final business structure*

As mentioned earlier,

☐ *Get a business email address*

Once you set up your domain name, hosting account, and website, you'll be able to configure a few business email addresses. Suggestions: yourname@mycompany.com, orders@mycompany.com, feedback@mycompany.com

☐ *Get business cards/letterhead/brochures*

If you conduct business predominantly in the physical world, or if you meet potential clients face to face, or attend conferences, it may be wise to get physical business cards, letterhead and brochures for distribution. Otherwise, in this increasingly digital age, it's not an immediate requirement.

☐ *Design a logo*

This would be a good investment. I previously used Gotlogos.com, but as of 2014, they seem to be no longer in business. 99Designs is bit more expensive, but the concept seems great! You submit your design request along with payment, and the design process run as a contest where multiple designers submit their designs and compete for your decision. I think I'll give that one a try on my next new project!

☐ *Set up office space or physical location*

There are some situations in which having a physical business location or storefront, or meeting site is necessary. Inventory storage, product display, workshops, demonstration, meetings, etc., may require it. However, in this digital age and work-at-home freedom, there's really no need to invest in this in advance unless absolutely necessary.

23. ❑ Recap ❑

We've set up a basic structure that will allow people to contact you and send you money. We've focused on the critical elements. If you were to do nothing else but send a pre-sell announcement requesting payment, you'd have everything you need to start making money…even if you didn't have a product!

SECTION: YOUR PRODUCT

*Product not created yet? Read Chapter 7 in **Turn Your Passion into Profit***

24. ❑ Understand what a product is ❑

> **Product**: *A high quality object or service, in the hands of a consumer, in exchange for something of value.*

I share this definition of a product to emphasize that it's not a product until there is value exchanged for it. In practical terms, it is often money that will be exchanged for the thing of value you are offering. However, it could easily be exchanged for another product or service (i.e. barter)

25. ❑ Ask the right product development questions ❑

A major part of the quick start process lies in coming up with the right product. You need to think about your assets and talents in a unique way in order to see the value in them, and in order to arrange and organize it correctly. This, perhaps, is the part that can't be taught (and for which my clients pay me to coach them). However, here are a few questions I ask myself when I approach a new object or service with potential:

❑ Can I break up this product in multiple parts and sell each one separately?

❑ Can I release each part on a regular basis and create a subscription product?

❑ Can this be sold in multiple formats (books, cds, video)?

26. ❑ Test your product idea ❑

You need to assess whether your product idea is really of high quality and ultimately in demand by the consumer. The best way, of course, is to test it in some way. If you're not able to test it, then are others successfully selling a somewhat similar product upon which you can base your potential success? One of the best ways to test it is to pre-sell it. More on that later.

27. ❑ Design cover, packaging, label for your product/service ❑

Investing in professional product design is worthwhile expenditure. Sometimes you can sell a product simply on how it appears!

28. ❏ Price your product/service appropriately ❏

A general "rule of thumb" for profitability in mail order is to price your product no less than five times the cost of production. (Newsflash! If you're selling your product online for physical deliver in the real world, you're in the mail order business!) In other words, if it costs $1.00 to manufacture your product, you should sell it at no less than $5.00 if you are to make a profit. Remember, there are expenses, overhead costs, delivery and a wholesale cost (the price you sell it to stores) that you have to factor into your final retail price.

29. ❏ Create samples and mock-ups of your product ❏

Creating a sample of your product has the proven, yet still mysterious and magical effect of helping bring it to reality faster! Whenever I would write a new book, I would first find a book from the store or library that was the approximate page count and trim size I wanted my book to be. I would create a mockup cover which included *"Title…by Walt Goodridge"* to wrap this library book. I would walk around with this prototype, and place it on my desk or shelf so I could envision the future manifestation of my own book.

30. ❏ Establish a manufacturing and delivery system ❏

Make sure you have a system in place to manufacture and deliver your product or service. My assumption for this manual, is that you have a book, CD or video manufactured and fulfilled by CreateSpace™ (See "The Case for CreateSpace" in Appendix)

31. ❏ Launch the "first edition" of product/service ❏

Think "quick start." Think of this as the first edition or "version 1.0," of your product or invention. It may go through several upgrades in the process of achieving perfection. If applicable, offer digital *and* physical versions of product.

32. ❏ Sell or pre-sell your product or service ❏

Now, here's where we get to the essence of the quick start philosophy and strategy. You don't need to have everything in place in order to start generating real money for your product or service. You can start *pre-selling* at any point during this process. Even your "coming soon" website page can generate money for you! For tips on how to think, refer back to "Separating Unconnected Events."

Start now by sending out a "coming soon, please order now" announcement to your immediate network of contacts.

SECTION: YOUR WEB PRESENCE

The details of creating a website that sells are covered in-depth in Websites That Sell. However, here are the essential steps.

33. ❑ Reserve the "best" domain name ❑

The very first thing I do with any new project or idea is decide how I'm going to sell it online. So, coming up with the best domain name (your "dot com") is a critical first step.

You need a domain name people can spell, remember and share easily with their friends. Make sure you reserve the DOT COM for your particular domain. (i.e. owning only the dot NET, Dot Org, or any other domain extension is not good enough.) See FAQ in Appendix for tips on choosing a domain name)

34. ❑ Set up a web presence/hosting account ❑

To establish your web presence, you need a company to "host" your site You can use www.1and1.com to sign up for a "home" or a "business" account. The rates are great and there's usually a "50% off for the first 6 months" promotion offer. (Home account: 6.99 or Business account: 9.99/month)
OPTION 2: You could also simply set up a free blog using Blogger.com or Wordpress.org, or simply use a Facebook account. However, it is still more professional to sell products through a website with a unique domain name.

1and1 Notes:
You don't need a domain name to set up the 1and1 hosting account, so you could even do this first.
1. Visit 1and1.com, find "web hosting" link
2. Choose "beginner" or "home" or "business" account
3. Choose any of the optional (for a fee) security/additional features
4. Enter domain name or select "add domain name later"
5. Pay for first 6 months; refundable in 90 days.
6. Choose country
7. Complete owner information
8. Choose password
9. Pay for hosting! You're done! You now have a hosting account!

• It takes anywhere from a few minutes to 48 hours for your domain to "propagate" throughout the worldwide internet system to be reachable.
• Either 1and1's "Beginner" or "Home" account is sufficient. However, keep in mind that most shopping carts require a MySQL database. So, when choosing a hosting company account, select an option that offers such a database.

35. ❑ Set up a "shopping cart" ❑

A shopping cart is the most convenient way for your customers to complete the checkout process, AND gives you the flexibility to easily add more products as your business grows.

OPTION 1: Since Paypal® offers a shopping cart, you could save a little time and energy by simply adding the necessary Paypal HTML code to your website rather than invest in a shopping cart at this time.

36. ❑ Create a website that sells ❑

My *Websites That Sell* manual has a thorough step-by-step checklist for creating a website that sells. Here, however, are some key items to include:

❑ testimonials
❑ image of your product
❑ contact Information, address, telephone number
❑ guarantee
❑ shipping costs
❑ physical address for customers who wish to mail check/money order
❑ fax number for customers who wish to fax orders
❑ feedback/join form

37. ❑ Create additional web presence and social networks ❑

Stay current with the latest social media networks and determine which are good fits for your product or service.

❑ Set up a Facebook™ page for yourself
❑ Start a Facebook™ Group
❑ Start a Twitter™ account
❑ Start an Instagram™ account
❑ Set up a LinkedIn™ Account
❑ Post videos to Youtube and include links back to your site
❑ Advertise your product on eBay

38. ❑ Test the final version of your site and launch ❑

Make sure everything looks and works well in different browsers and at different internet access speeds from dialup to DSL!

SECTION: ACCEPTING MONEY

You MUST make it easy for customers to send you their money.

39. ❑ Accept credit cards ❑

Whether you have a "brick & mortar" (i.e. physical) store or just a web presence, you must be able to accept credit/debit cards for payment for your product or service. You can apply to become a VISA/Mastercard merchant through traditional means (i.e. your bank), or you can use Paypal (as previously discussed)

40. ❑ Provide a PDF order form❑

There are folks who will prefer to order by fax or "snail mail" (the on-land mail delivery service) even after visiting your website. Offer them a downloadable/printable order form they can fax or mail to you. Remember to include your physical mailing address on the form.

41. ❑ Accept credit cards in person w/mobile phone ❑

It's called a mobile transaction device. You may have seen such gadgets in action if you attend trade shows and conventions,

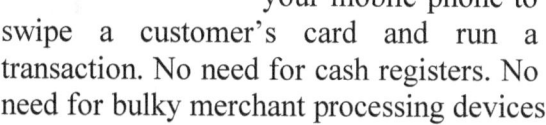 or if you've shopped in any Apple store. It requires an app to be installed in your mobile phone, and allows you to use your mobile phone to  swipe a customer's card and run a transaction. No need for cash registers. No need for bulky merchant processing devices.

Review of Payal Here: http://www.mobiletransaction.org/paypal-here-review-us/

42. ❑ Add optional payment methods ❑

Be sure to be able to accept check by phone, bank wire, COD for your product/service. Also, be sure to have your name as well as your business name and other "dbas" (doing business as trade names) on your checking account so that customers may make checks payable to each.

43. ❑ Review your progress ❑

Here's where we are after completing the previous steps:

• Your domain name has been reserved and is active.

• Your initial site has been designed, uploaded and accessible on the internet via the domain name you reserved. (If you followed the steps in the "Websites That Sell" Manual, it could already be fully designed and functional at this point, or you could simply have a "coming soon" page which includes a brief overview of your product, a launch date, and a "pre-order now" option so you can start pre-selling your product.

• Your Paypal™ account is in place and configured to accept any pre-payments.

• You are using the Paypal™ or the X-Cart shopping cart.

• If not already created, your product is going through the Createspace™ submission, review and proof approval process.

We can now go back and "fill in the blanks" in the full process by going through the Ultimate Checklist which follows. However, at this point, you have been officially "Quick Started" and could make your first sale at any moment!

In order to encourage that first sale as quickly as possible, we shall set some goals and then execute something called the Condition Formula for Non-Existence.

SECTION: SETTING GOALS

44. ❑ Read about Achieving Goals ❑

The achievement of one's goals, no matter how large or small the endeavor, relies on goals, purposes and activities being aligned and organized.

A goal is not something that one decides upon which then miraculously comes to fruition, just because one decided it would. The attainment of a goal necessitates that certain actions be carried out in the real world which effect some change for the better and a step closer toward its accomplishment.

One can be working toward a goal, but discover that his actions do not yield any forward progress. This occurs not only for an individual in his life, but also for an organization, state or country of any size. This can be a result of the plans, actions and other factors not being aligned to attain the goal.

There are actually a number of subjects that make up any activity. Each of these must operate in a coordinated manner to achieve success in the intended accomplishment of the envisioned goal.

GOALS: A goal is a known objective toward which actions are directed with the purpose of achieving that end.

PURPOSES: A purpose is a lesser goal applying to specific activities or subjects. It often expresses future intentions.

POLICY: Policy consists of the operational rules or guides for the organization which are not subject to change.

PLANS: A plan is a short-range broad intention thought up for the handling of a broad area to remedy it or expand it, or to obstruct or impede an opposition to expansion.

PROGRAMS: A program is a series of steps in sequence to carry out a plan.

PROJECTS: A project is a sequence of steps written to carry out one step of a program.

ORDERS: An order is a verbal or written direction to carry out a program step or apply general policy.

IDEAL SCENES: An ideal scene expresses what a scene or area ought to be. If one has not envisioned an ideal scene with which to compare the existing scene, he will not be able to recognize departures from it.

STATISTIC: A statistic is a number or amount compared to an earlier number or amount of the same thing. Statistics refer to the quantity of work done or the value of it.

VALUABLE FINAL PRODUCTS: A valuable final product is a product that can be exchanged for the services or goods of the society.

(Excerpt from Targets And Goals by L. Ron Hubbard)

45. ❑ Review my Goal-Achieving SAMPLE ❑

Here is a sample of how I used the template to achieve the promotion of increase exposure and sales my own product.

GOAL: To increase sales of my *Living True To Your Self* book.

SITUATION: All the advanced reviews and feedback so far indicate that this is a unique book many people would find insightful, informative and entertaining. There is tremendous untapped potential here. I want to achieve massive sales and global reach for the book and its concept.

PURPOSE: Establish myself nationally as a self-help guru, and best-selling author, increase sales of all my products, improve my standard of living, and achieve even higher levels of financial independence and fame.

STRATEGIC PLAN: The plan is to use my existing channels as well as my existing reputation and nomadpreneur accomplishments to market the book.
- Include an announcement page and reference it in all my existing products.
- Publish *Living True to Your Self* articles and excerpts
- Conduct teleclasses and virtual workshops once the book is released
- Promote to my existing mailing lists
- Target book clubs; speaker assoc; mlm companies/gurus etc.
- Target *Passion* and *Game* to correctional facilities and military

Major Target: (broad general ambition)
      1. To increase national attention for me and my products
      2. To achieve sales of 100 copies per day

Primary Targets: (organizational, personnel and communication steps)
      1. Set up Team Tour, Media friends and Gatekeepers

Vital Targets: (essential for operation at all)
      1. Keep websites up and running at all times
      2. Keep supply of books replenished at all times
      3. Maintain cash flow and cash-on-hand
      4. Have media kit and video ready and available

Conditional Targets: (gather data about if, where and how a project can be done, then take action)
      1. Find out what daily sales are required to reach Amazon Top 10

Operating Targets: (directions, actions, schedule or timetable)
(PROMOTE via Listings, Press Releases, Articles, Advertising, Workshops)
- Set up new title with Createspace
- Contact Entrepreneur Magazine re: available for interview
    - Contact Entrepreneur Magazine again re: writing articles
    - Advertise on Careerbuilder.com
    - Advertise in Selfgrowth.com newsletter
- Send copy to Oprah Show & Magazine
- Use BlackPRWeb for press release distribution
- Use PRweb for press release
- Create inflight magazine query; submit to inflight magazines
- Prepare submission for Speaker Bureaus
    - read and implement Google adwords optimization/tracking tips
    (This is just a sample of the dozens of tasks in this section)

Ideal Scene:

   In my ideal scene, thousands of people each week purchase the book through Amazon and/or through my own site. My inbox is flooded with Online Order emails every day! My bank account grows from daily deposits. Orders are fulfilled quickly and customers return to the site frequently. In my ideal scene, visitors to my site number in the thousands daily. They order books and e-books and other products. Using my philosophy and formula, a movement of passionpreneurs living true to themselves is created. The book is an Amazon as well as a New York Times bestseller. It has been translated into 20 languages. I receive invitations from around the world to read and discuss it with fans. Book clubs use my books to spark interesting debates. Other life coaches and career counselors use it in their own practices. It has become the hottest new thing in inspiration and self-help. People are talking about it everywhere!

END OF SAMPLE

Goal Achieving Notes:
• Listen to or read the *Science of Getting Rich* by Wallace Wattles
(I have a free version of this available for download for members of my mailing list. Join at www.passionprofit.com)
• With each step forward, determine what you want to have happen next in your journey, and then think thoughts, develop strategy, say the words and take the actions to make it happen!

46. ❏ Complete YOUR OWN Goal-Achieving Template ❏
The following is a goal-achieving template you can use for any goal.

MAJOR Program:

Situation: _____

Purpose:_____

Major Target: (broad general ambition)
    1. My broad general ambition is to….

Primary Targets: (organizational, personnel, communication steps)
    1. _____
    2. _____
    3. _____

Vital Targets: (essential for operation at all)
    1. _____
    2. _____
    3. _____

Conditional Targets: (gather data about if, where and how a project can be done, then go into action)
    1. _____
    2. _____
    3. _____

Operating Targets: (directions, actions, schedule or timetable)
    1. _____
    2. _____
    3. _____

Production Targets: (set quantities for statistics)
    1. _____
    2. _____
    3. _____

Valuable Final Product & Ideal Scene
My valuable final product is _____

Ideal Scene: In my ideal scene: _____

SECTION: PREPARING FOR LAUNCH & PROMOTION

47. ❑ Review the list of "chosen people" ❑

Review the list of "chosen people" in *Turn Your Passion Into Profit*, and decide who the target audience will be for your product or service.

48. ❑ Set official launch 2 months from now ❑

We need to have a concrete date in mind that we can aim for. We will share this date with others so they, too, will have a date to visit the site, place their orders or perform whatever action you request of them.

49. ❑ Make a comprehensive list of keywords ❑

What words would people type into a search engine in order to find your product or service? Open a text editor file or Word document and start compiling this list. Knowing these key words will be very important as you perform the next several tasks.

50. ❑ Find/develop a winning headline ❑

See 300 of the best headlines ever written at http://www.passionprofit.com/wts/300bestheadlines/

51. ❑ Write sales copy for your product/service ❑

See *Websites that Sell* for an effective sales copy template.

52. ❑ Write press release announcing your product ❑

See *Appendix* for a sample press release.

53. ❑ Write "Available for Interview" announcement ❑

It's a simple announcement that shows your area of expertise, and why the media person's audience will find you an entertaining guest to be interviewed. See a sample at www.waltgoodridge.com/

54. ❑ Write articles and mention your product or service ❑

Become an "expert" for your issues relating to your target niche. Write articles and include a mention of your website/product in the bio of the article.

55. ❑ Develop 25-word (short) & 50-word (long) sales blurb ❑

As you start to list, register and promote your business/site/product on different websites, you'll discover that some of the forms on these sites have specific character counts that limit the size of your headline, press release, content and author/company bio. You can prepare for this by creating a short and long version of your sales pitch.

56. ❑ Start capturing emails and accumulating "friends" ❑

Even with the almost total dominance of social networks, I still prefer "ancient" email as a mode of communication. Grow your network with both, and don't rely solely on your Facebook or Twitter following as a way to maintain contact with your network. Who knows, there may even be a day in which people start to boycott Facebook and actually return to cultivating friendships in real time with real people!

57. ❑ Set up Google Alerts for your chosen keywords ❑

A Google "alert" is a way to monitor the internet. The Google.com search engine provides a feature and service whereby you can receive an email notice any time a website or blog posts a story or release containing a specific keyword.

For example, let's say you have a business that relates to dog grooming. You set up a Google alert for the key word "dog grooming" and whenever a forum discussion, blog post, personal or business website, eBay listing, Amazon product etc appears on the internet with the words "dog grooming" a notice with a synopsis of the post along with an extract of how paragraph/sentence in which the key word appears is created and sent to you.

SECTION: IMPLEMENT NON-EXISTENCE FORMULA

This next section, as simple as it may appear, is perhaps the most important part of the quick start process. I define a quick start as the speed with which you go from idea to first sale. Now that you've (a) established the business structure, and (b) created the channels for people to send you money for the product or service of value you've created, and (c) prepared what you want to say to communicate that value, now is when you (d) actually start to communicate that value to others in order to encourage them to complete the exchange of money for value.

58. ❏ Understand the Non-Existence Formula ❏

The Non Existence Formula is the first of several proven "condition formulas" designed to grow your business sales (or any venture) up from zero to tremendous success! There are four (4) phases in the Non-Existence Formula:

1. FIND THE COMMUNICATION LINES
2. MAKE YOURSELF KNOWN
3. FIND OUT WHAT IS NEEDED OR WANTED
4. DO, PRODUCE AND/OR DELIVER IT.

(For the full set of Condition Formulas designed to take your business all the way to a condition of "Power", see Turn Your Passion Into Profit)

59. ❑ Start compiling the lines of communication ❑

In each industry (publishing, entertainment, fashion, etc.), there exist certain key organizations, vendors, suppliers, customers, clients, media, television shows, member organizations, etc. with whom you will be communicating. Make a comprehensive list of all of these by answering:

☐ Who needs to know about my product/service?
☐ Where should my product/service be heard/read about/reviewed?
☐ Who are the leaders in my industry/area of expertise?
☐ Who are the gatekeepers in my industry/area of expertise?
☐ What international markets exist for my product?
☐ Who are the recognized experts who should review my product?
☐ Review the list of "chosen people" in Turn Your Passion Into Profit

60. ❑ Review this list for even more ideas ❑

Here is a list of gatekeepers and gathering places that may make unique additions to your Comm. Lines and marketing strategies:

☐ gas stations   ☐ associations   ☐ QVC, HSN, etc.
☐ cruise lines   ☐ book clubs   ☐ catalog companies
☐ travel agents   ☐ schools   ☐ foundations
☐ airline magazines ☐ universities   ☐ Public radio
☐ hospitals   ☐ podcasts
☐ auto mechanics   ☐ internet cafes
☐ charities   ☐ MLM companies
☐ public speakers   ☐ maid service companies

61. ❏ Review these industries for still more comm lines ❏

- ☐ Advertising Agencies
- ☐ Apparel Stores
- ☐ Auto Dealerships
- ☐ Auto Parts Stores
- ☐ Computers Wholesale
- ☐ Consumer Services
- ☐ Department Stores
- ☐ Discount, Variety Stores
- ☐ Drug Stores
- ☐ Electronics Stores
- ☐ Electronics Wholesale
- ☐ Food Wholesale
- ☐ Gaming Activities
- ☐ Grocery Stores
- ☐ Home Furnishing Stores
- ☐ Home Improvement Stores
- ☐ Jewelry Stores
- ☐ Lodging
- ☐ Management Services
- ☐ Marketing Services
- ☐ Medical Equipment
- ☐ Movie Production, Theaters
- ☐ Music & Video Stores
- ☐ Regional Airlines
- ☐ Rental & Leasing Services

- ☐ Research Services
- ☐ Resorts & Casinos
- ☐ Restaurants
- ☐ Security Services
- ☐ Shipping
- ☐ Specialty Eateries
- ☐ Specialty Retail, Other
- ☐ Sporting Activities
- ☐ Sporting Goods Stores
- ☐ Staffing Services
- ☐ Technical Services
- ☐ Toy & Hobby Stores
- ☐ Trucking
- ☐ Utility companies

62. ❏ Ask the right target market questions ❏

As important as asking the right questions to determine *what* to sell and how to sell it, is asking the right questions to determine *who* to sell to.

☐ Who else could benefit from this product if I change it slightly?

☐ Does this have any government or military applications?

☐ Would any large organizations with huge memberships be interested?

☐ Could this be sold on shelves in stores?

63. ❑ Start making your list of comm lines ❑

PUBLICITY
❑ 5 Blogs related to your product/service topic
1. _____   4. _____
2. _____   5. _____
3. _____

❑ 5 Online communities/forums related to your area of expertise
1. _____   4. _____
2. _____   5. _____
3. _____

❑ 5 Industry magazines incl. editors and specific writers/reporters
1. _____   4. _____
2. _____   5. _____
3. _____

❑ 5 Television or cable shows which cover your topic
1. _____   4. _____
2. _____   5. _____
3. _____

❑ 5 Local, regional and national newspapers
1. _____   4. _____
2. _____   5. _____
3. _____

❑ 5 Article Distribution sites
1. _____   4. _____
2. _____   5. _____
3. _____

RETAIL/WHOLESALE DISTRIBUTION:
❑ 5 Stores/Supermarkets
1. _____   4. _____
2. _____   5. _____
3. _____

☐ 5 Specialty shops to send product announcements

1. _____ 4. _____
2. _____ 5. _____
3. _____

☐ 5 Wholesalers/Distributors that supply the stores/supermarkets

1. _____ 4. _____
2. _____ 5. _____
3. _____

BULK ORDERS

☐ 5 Clubs, Organizations, Corporations that might purchase in bulk

1. _____ 4. _____
2. _____ 5. _____
3. _____

☐ 5 Government agencies that might need your product/service

1. _____ 4. _____
2. _____ 5. _____
3. _____

☐ 5 Libraries/Library systems that might carry your product

1. _____ 4. _____
2. _____ 5. _____
3. _____

KEEP ADDDING TO ALL OF THESE LISTS! THERE'S ALWAYS
SOMEONE TO CONTACT AND SOMETHING TO DO!

64. ❏ Make yourself known ❏

Your next task is to make the people on your list aware of your existence. Once you create your marketing materials, brochures, website, sales letters, press release, etc. you will then use them to make yourself known to the world.

Using your list of communication lines:

☐ Launch your marketing campaign
☐ Start by sending an announcement email to friends and family
☐ Send press release or product announcement to your Comm Lines
☐ Send regular emails to your list
☐ Post comments on others' blogs
☐ Submit articles to various sites and engines
☐ Post to your social network sites
☐ Send out review copies/samples of your product
☐ Attend trade shows and conventions

65. ❏ Find out what is needed or wanted ❏

Each of those lines of communication has certain requirements for you to do business with, join, purchase and/or promote to them. Your mission is to find out how the game is played and what you need to be, do and have in order to win!

☐ Conduct surveys of your visitors and customers
☐ Follow-up with visitors who abandon their shopping carts
☐ Keep an on-going list of what people email and ask for

66. ❏ Deliver what is needed or wanted ❏

Once you know what people want, give it to them!

☐ Implement practical customer suggestions
☐ Develop new products based on customers' requests
☐ Provide content (articles, excerpts, press releases) to media outlets

67. ❏ Make your first sale! ❏

I can't guarantee when it will happen, but if you've followed all the steps, and have a product people want, it will happen! And, when it does, proceed to step 68!

68. ❏ Rejoice! ❏

69. ❏ Conduct a follow-up survey of your first customer! ❏

How did she hear about you? What prompted her to buy? Was she satisfied with the product? What might be done to improve it?

SECTION: ONGOING OPERATIONS
Ongoing tasks based on my own business model

70. ❏ Promote your site and business offline ❏

Never leave home without samples of your product and brochures. (Yes, even to the beach!) Constantly envision, talk about, promote, market and expose yourself, your product and your website to everyone you meet.

71. ❏ Promote your site and business online ❏

☐ OPTION: Use as a service like addpro.com to register your site with many search engines, or register with each search engine on your own

☐ OPTION: Use a PR Distribution company like Prweb.com to announce your company or product to the industry

72. ❏ Create new products ❏

You should not rely on a single product/service or target audience as the basis of your business. Think of new products, or of slightly modified versions of existing products that could be sold to slightly different audiences.

73. ❏ Advertise online ❏

Use Google's Adword Program to launch a keyword campaign
- No money is needed to start the campaign.
- You pay only for clicks received, possibly as little as 5 cents per click.
- Your card will be billed at the end of the month.

74. ❏ Do in-person appearances ❏

Speaking engagements, demonstrations and teleclasses.

75. ❏ Constantly streamline your operations ❏

There are always ways to make your sites load faster, make your emails get through spam filters, to increase inquiry-to-sale conversion rates, and generally increase the efficiency and profitability of your venture!

SECTION: DAILY TASKS

76. ❏ Check and respond to email ❏

77. ❏ Get feedback from your customers ❏
      Consider using surveymonkey.com to conduct customer surveys.

78. ❏ Charge customer credit cards ❏

79. ❏ Prepare and fill orders ❏

80. ❏ Send out brochures ❏

81. ❏ Check website stats ❏

82. ❏ Post comments on blogs and articles ❏

SECTION: WEEKLY TASKS

83. ❏ Communicate with subscribers ❏

84. ❏ Trade ads and links with other entrepreneurs ❏

SECTION: MONTHLY TASKS

85. ❏ Pay bills ❏
      Pay rent/utilities, voicemail, eFax, Paypal™ merchant account fees.

SECTION: QUARTERLY & ANNUAL TASKS

86. ❏ File state/city taxes and federal income tax ❏

87. ❏ Renew domain registrations ❏

88. ❏ Renew PO Boxes, licenses, SSL Certificates ❏

SECTION: BUSINESS GROWTH STRATEGY

Your overall strategy for success should be to:
Create Assets
Increase Site Traffic & Accumulate Subscribers
Generate Media Exposure
Grow an Affiliate Network
Increase placement in retail outlets/distribution outlets

89. ❏ Create assets ❏

Each of the items you create and publish represents an income stream that can create passive, residual income for years to come. The first book I published in 1992 (*Rap; This Game of Exposure*, now called *Change the Game*) is still my company's best selling item.

90. ❏ Increase site traffic and accumulate subscribers ❏

The power and success of your direct online sales generation campaign rests in the size and loyalty of your online mailing list. You will generate new subscribers through keyword advertising in major search engines, word-of-mouth referrals. Giving away something for free on your site is a good way to collect subscribers. Maintain contact with your subscribers through a weekly email newsletter.

91. ❏ Generate media exposure ❏

My most successful campaigns have been reviews in newspapers. Next have been endorsements from key people. Generate reviews in magazines, articles and websites. This legitimizes your in the consumer's mind. A continuing Public Relations Campaign is critical to achieving your objectives.

92. ❑ Grow affiliate network ❑

Through my experience in network marketing, I realize word-of-mouth marketing is the most powerful form of advertising. An affiliate program is the best way to give existing customers an incentive to do your marketing for you.

93. ❑ Focus on retail sales ❑

To maximize sales and to reach audiences who may not be browsing online, you will also need a focused strategy to get your products into retail outlets if appropriate.

SECTION: PREFERRED VENDORS & METHODS

I've been online since 1997. All those years of searching for the easiest, cheapest and most efficient, user-friendly options have resulted in the following preferred vendors list for various aspects of my business operations as well as those of my coaching clients. There are, of course, many other options available. Note: I earn no commissions from these vendors.

TIP: Of course, you are not obligated to use the vendors I recommend for hosting, domain registration, etc. However, one good reason for doing so is that if we ever work together, or if you have a question, I will be able to help you quite quickly as I'll be familiar with how these companies systems are set up.

94. ❑ Consider these vendors, platforms and software ❑

Advertising Income I generate income by placing ads on my websites using the following providers/agents. See The Websites That Sell Manual for other advertising income strategies.	**TextLinkBrokers.cm** **Linkworth.com** **Text-link-ads.com**

Blogging Because Blogger.com is owned by Google, blog posts on a Blogger.com blog seem to show up in Google's search engine faster.	**Wordpress.com** **Blogger.com**

Book writing I write my books in my Mac's Textedit word processor, then import to Word™ I use PS2PDF to convert it to PDF format for upload to CreateSpace™	**TextEdit (Mac)** **Microsoft Word™**

Book/CD/Video Manufacturing I now use CreateSpace.com to manufacture my books, cds and videos. (See "The Case for CreateSpace" in Appendix)	**CreateSpace.com**

Bulletin Board Create a community feel for your website. If you want an even simpler way to launch the phpbb bulletin board, check out phpbb88, they host it for you and save you all the configuration headaches.	**Phpbb.com (Free)** **Phpbb88.com**

Conference Calls In order to host conference calls with my lists of subscribers and customers, I use FreeConferencecall.com	**FreeConferencecall.com** **MrConference.com** **(FREE)**

Email Distribution In order to communicate with my lists of subscribers and customers, I use a combination of free programs as well as customized in-house programs.	**Subscribeme.com** **Phplist.com** **Customized** **(FREE)**

Fax I previously used Efax.com™ However, as the need for faxes has decreased, I now use Myfax.com	**MyFax.com/free** **EFax.com**

Images and Graphics I use a stock photo agency to get images for my book covers. A great image is often half the design. Alamy has royalty-free as well as paid images you can use.	**Alamy.com** **123RF.com**

Domain Registration Anytime I come up with a new domain name idea, I reserve it for only $10.10 per year through Powerpipe.com. I've since found options about a buck or two cheaper, but Powerpipe's control panel is more user-friendly, and URL forwarding is included in their price.	**1and1.com** **Bluehost.com**

Keyword generation and research To find out what keywords might be effective for my marketing, I use Google's keyword tool. https://adwords.google.com/select/KeywordToolExternal	**Adwords.Google** *(requires Google account)*

List Management Manage your lists. Send autoresponders. Send announcements.	**Wordpress**

Logo Design I previously used Gotlogos.com for designs, but as of 2014, they seem to be out of business.	**Elance.com** **99designs.com**

Merchant Processing After years of using a variety of merchant processing companies, I settled on, and am quite happy with Paypal™. Paypal has a virtual terminal feature, which means you don't have to have and pay for a physical terminal machine.	**Paypal.com** **($30/month** + 2.2% - 2.9% + $0.30 USD per transaction **)**
Shopping Cart There are many shopping carts on the market. I have used Cubecart (an open source) easy to install and FREE system in the past, but now use X-Cart.com	**X-Cart.com** **Cubecart.com (FREE)**
Software (Miscellaneous) I use Photoshop™ to design my book covers	**Adobe Photoshop**
SSL Certificate If you follow my advice, 1and1 will offer you a Geotrust SSL certificate for a yearly fee of $49 that will be already incorporated into your hosting account	**GeoTrust through 1and1.com ($49/year)**
Tracker Keep track of visitors to your site with this free software. Requires minimal knowledge of HTML.	**Extremetracking.com (FREE)**
Voicemail In order to facilitate my nomadpreneur lifestyle, I use a voice mail service to take incoming calls.	**Google Voice (FREE)**
Website Hosting Most of my sites are hosted by 1and1.com	**1and1.com**

THOUSANDS of dollars in savings are possible using the vendors and methods I've recommended above. Along with the right product and service (priced appropriately), there's absolutely no reason you can't turn your unique passion into real profits!

95. ❑ Read my thoughts on true freedom and options ❑

After sharing with you the various vendors and software and strategies I recommend, this seems like the appropriate place to say a few words about freedom and options. So, let's step back a bit and look at this whole thing as objectively and as dispassionately as we can.

The whole reason we're doing all of this to quick start our business is to achieve a certain amount of financial reward in order to create independence and freedom. However, I don't want you to get so caught up in the pursuit and the paradigm that you don't see the contradictions and traps that inherently exist.

The goal should not be to get "more and more and more." Why not? Because the more things you acquire, is the less free you are. Freedom comes from detachment from the pursuit of things. The more you believe you MUST have the latest iteration of smart phone, is the more bound you are to have to work to get it.

Another trap I wish to warn you of is getting too comfortable with the status quo. Just because everyone is using a particular platform/software/product, doesn't mean it's the right choice for you. People are starting to see how Paypal colludes with the government to shut down the accounts of government whistleblowers. They see how Facebook sells their information and disrespects their privacy and censors their posts. They see how certain browsers steal their personal information. In other words, they see that there is actually a *reduction* in freedom the more they buy into what everyone else is doing.

As a result, there are other options to those I have suggested in this and other manuals:

There are browsers (eg. Tor) that offer greater privacy and anonymity.

There are countries (eg. Sweden) that offer better banking secrecy laws.

There are social media platforms (eg. Diasp.eu, Unseen.is) that offer decentralized storage of information, privacy and that don't censor your posts.

There are payment processors that exist as options to the big ones.

As an entrepreneur marketing to the public, you need to know "what everyone is doing." However, keep your eyes open. Don't get too caught up in the status quo and the paradigm of "more money! more money! more money" that you can't see how the pursuit itself may actually be infringing on true freedom.

SECTION: FINAL WORDS

With that, I've given you pretty much all the information I have in the way of strategy and technique for quick starting your business. The rest is up to you and your willingness and commitment to implement. To get you on your way, let me offer a few final words of encouragement.

96. ❏ Understand how to achieve anything you desire ❏

"Courage is discipline in the face of fear.
Discipline is courage in the face of distraction."

Many people will try to sell you on quick and easy strategies to do just about anything in life--everything from losing weight to making money to having a better sex life. They wish to sell you the magic pill or fairy dust that will work like a charm. Processes may be simple. Specific techniques may be easy. Strategies may work like magic. Certain environments may be more conducive to success. However, there is often something missing from these formulas.

It is my belief and experience that you can achieve just about anything you desire in life if you have courage and discipline. It takes discipline to achieve happiness. It takes discipline to make money through a website that sells. That's what it all boils down to. Courage and discipline are the interchangeable, complementary and inextricably linked sides of the same coin. Any solution that suggests otherwise is doing you a disservice.

The good news is you can develop these traits regardless of all the inner and outer challenges you believe you face.

Courage is discipline in the face of fear.

Discipline is courage in the face of distraction.

Once you are introduced to the possibility of a new reality (for example, that you can make money through a website that sells) with different belief system, and a different set of choices, required actions, consequences and benefits, it requires COURAGE to choose to embark on that reality in the face of inertia and fear and habit, society's norms and the opinions of others. Furthermore, once you have actually embarked on the new path, it requires DISCIPLINE to maintain and sustain those actions in the face of inertia and fear and habit and distraction and derision.

To quick start your business, you need:

The courage to believe something new about yourself.
The courage to believe something new about how to make money.
The courage to take the action steps to launch your business.
The discipline to keep monitoring and tweaking your business/products.
The discipline to keep trying new products and strategies.

The courage to start. The discipline to continue. That, in my opinion, is what it requires to achieve anything you desire!

97. ❑ Read my ultimate quick start success secrets! ❑

I'd also like to share with you why I'm able to get so much accomplished in a short period of time. (This is an essential trait for quick start success.)

I work from lists

I think the biggest secret is that I work from lists. Whenever I get any thought worthy of implementation—or for that matter, *any* thought that might be worthy of implementation, I stop whatever I am doing (even getting out of the shower) to write it down. I may add the idea it to my daily task list, or to a task list of a specific project. (I always have several Textedit™ files open on my screen to which I can add new ideas/tasks whenever they come to me). It's not unusual for my daily task list to have 50-100 things that need to get done. I include *everything*! I start each day compiling the list, and continually add to it during the day. As a result of honing this discipline, I've discovered a few things:

(a) writing things down "empties" my mind of each incoming idea, frees my mind to allow in even more new ideas! With my mind relieved of having to expend the mental energy to attempt to remember everything, I can be more creative, sleep better whenever I rest!

(b) I can see the big picture and organize the tasks in sequential order

I leave nothing to chance (or memory)

When I work with others, I leave nothing to chance. One of my pet peeves when I hear a voicemail message is hearing the caller end with the phrase *"you've got my number (or email). Get back to me!"*

Aaargh! That's a recipe for failure and disappointment. What if the person you're calling has lost their address/phone book? What if they're checking their voicemail from someone else's phone? What if they lost their computer or smart phone with all their contact information? What if they never even had your number written down anywhere, were always just recalling it from memory, but now have amnesia??? In any scenario, they now have to look up your contact information in order to get back to you. My point is that if you want someone to call you back, leave them a number. Every time.

I cover all the bases

Whenever I communicate with customers, I provide specific instructions, or a link for them to perform the specific action I'd like them to—even if I've provided the link or instructions in previous emails. Particularly if I'm answering questions leading up to a sale, I add a "p.s." that includes *"Here's the payment link: _____."* I make sure all the bases are covered.

I think for the other person

This is essentially the art of selling: thinking like your potential customer. However, it can be manifested in many ways as you deal with clients, business associates, and just about everyone in life, especially if you're asking them to do a favor for you. Remember, people are more interested in themselves than in you. They've got their own issues and challenges, their own world views, their own motivations that determine how and when they act.

What's she going to need in order to do what I wish her to?

What sort of personal motivation does he have that I can relate to?

Let me give you a simple example. I am currently on the island of Saipan. I recently contacted a tour guide on the neighboring island of Guam for some information. I was in the process of arranging a tour of Guam for a potential client

It's a simple enough request that I'm sure he'd have no qualms about helping me with. However, I know I was asking for a favor. I know he's not in the business of hotel recommendations. And, even though he would ultimately benefit from the future customer (as he has in the past), I always want to think for—and on behalf of—the other person. So, after I sent the original request, I sent a follow-up email that said, *"by the way, feel free to suggest a hotel that's convenient for YOU, since you'll be the one picking up the client when they arrive on Guam." It shows I'm trying to make things easy for him. It gets him thinking about exactly which hotels are actually close to his business.*

These examples all fall in the category of *"how can I make things easy?"* I play the desired scenario in my mind, put myself in the position of the other person, play close attention to whatever tools, motivation they will require to perform the desired action, then fill in the blanks to make things easy

98. ❏ Read How to Win Friends...! ❏

I would recommend reading *How to Win Friends and Influence People* by Dale Carnegie, as your starting point for understanding yourself in relation to the rest of the world. This has essentially been the blueprint I follow in order to work well with others!

99. ❏ Congratulate yourself! ❏

I encourage you to commend yourself for taking this step in turning your passion into profit! According to statistics, 97% of the population works for someone else and will retire dependent on family, friends or the federal government for survival. Your willingness to envision and pursue something different for yourself, as well as the act of purchasing this manual and carving time out of your busy days to take yourself through it already sets you apart from the greater population. That's what makes you special.

I believe this specialness means you are GUARANTEED to be successful....provided you simply keep moving forward, changing course as necessary. And remember that, often, what you seek does not exist at the end of a simple straight line without curves and obstructions, but lies hidden in a maze in the middle of an obstacle course!

Decide from now that giving up is NOT an option. Whenever you encounter what you perceive are obstacles and failures, always ask yourself, "Given this situation, what can I do NOW to use it to my advantage and move me one step closer to my goals?"

So, again, congrats, best of success, and remember:

Success is a journey,
not a destination!

Walt F.J. Goodridge

100. ❏ Get started! ❏

p.s What's that? You've got questions? Well, keep reading!

DISCUSSIONS

Quick Start Discussion
Business Structure Discussion
Product Discussion
Accepting Money Discussion
Web Presence Discussion
Promotion Discussion
The Freedom Discussion
Final Words Discussion
The Case for CreateSpace™
Penny Power Marketing

DISCUSSION: Quick Start

Q: How quickly can I start making money?
A: HOW DOES 72 HOURS SOUND? Let me tell you a true story.

Once, on a Wednesday, a client and I were in his office brainstorming ways to harness his energy and expertise so that he might turn his passion into profit. A speaking tour? Great, but that would require too much time. A book? Good, but it wouldn't capture his personality. An audio CD? Bingo!

Here's what happened next:

On that same Wednesday, we brainstormed on what would be covered on the CD. I developed the press release, and he started securing press coverage using his PR contacts.

On Wednesday night, while he created the outline for the CD, I developed the website using the strategy in The "Websites That Sell" manual.

On Thursday, we brainstormed on an internet domain name, found one that was suitable and available, and we reserved it.

On Friday at 2:00am, the domain name activated and the site went "live."

On Friday at 9:00am, a mention of his site and product and sale price was sent to my mailing list of subscribers.

On Friday at 11:00pm we received our first order! (Remember the CD hadn't been recorded yet.)

On Monday, the audio was recorded in an exhausting, but exciting 12-hour session in a local studio.

On Tuesday, the order was shipped!

Q: How successful can I really be?
A: Honestly, you can be as successful as you expect to be. There are sites that earn a few dollars per day, sites that earn thousands per day, and other sites that earn millions! I can't guarantee what amount of money you'll make, but I can tell you that some of my own sites earn thousands monthly using the same techniques I'm sharing with you.

DISCUSSION: Business Structure

Q: What business structure should I choose?
A: That VARIES. Everyone's situation is different. However, you can read "Choosing The Right Business Structure" in *Turn Your Passion Into Profit*

Q: I have two lines of products--one for businesses and one for consumers. It would be nice to have a single name under whose umbrella the products to both businesses and those to consumers could be sold. The problem I'm running across is that any phrase that is great for one of them, is of mediocre appeal to the other. For example, "_____" is a great name for the business tools, but a bit of a stretch for the consumer crowd. And vice versa, any consumer-oriented names seem a little soft for business customers. So here are my questions.
1. Is it a problem to have two Paypal accounts for two different companies – one for the business products and one for the general masses?
2. How vital is a domain name for that company name?

A: There are two things you want to take into consideration:
1. What shows up on the customer's credit card statements as well their Paypal payment form and payment history, and
2. Who checks get written to

      If we brand "_____" as the name of the company on the website, then 30 or 60 days later when a customer happens to be reviewing his/her bank statement and they see a charge from "_____", they may not immediately recognize the charge and may dispute it. It happens a small percentage of the time, but it's usually better, I've found, to use a name that is recognizable by being somehow related to the product.

      Now, admittedly that's not always possible or practical, so the next best thing is to prepare the customer in advance for the appearance of the different name "Please note that charges to your card will appear on your statements as "_____" (That's what I do, and I make sure when the checkout process starts, that "The PassionProfit Company" appears on the shopping cart header)

      Who checks get written to:

      Not a major thing since your bank will probably allow multiple dbas, so you can tell your business customers "Make Checks Payable to: _____" and regular consumers can "Make Checks Payable to: _____"

Q: Can I have a business account if I don't have a business name?
A: Come on! It shouldn't take that long to come up with a business name. However, your bank should be able to set up a business account with your personal name, and you can amend the name on the account later. *(ie. Start as John Brown, then change to "John Brown dba Brown Arts." dba=doing business as)*

Q: Where can I get forms to set up my business?
A: Each state may require slight different forms. Your local Small Business Administration office can guide you. You can also ask at your bank. Some forms, (SS-4, for example) are available on the www.irs.gov site.

Q: Where do I get my Tax Id/EIN number?
A: Visit www.irs.gov, download Form SS-4, and call the number in the instructions to receive your EIN over the phone.

Q: Should I use my Social Security No. as my Tax Id No?
A: My suggestion is to get a separate EIN number by completing form SS-4.

Q: Should I get a "toll free" number?
A: These days, since long distance charges are as low as 4.9 cents/minute, offering a toll free number for your customers to reach you is not as much of an enticement as it once was. However, since it IS so cheap, you may wish to invest in one. It'll probably result in a few extra calls.

Q: Should I get a Mailboxes Etc™ mailbox?
A: I find that the US Postal Service PO box works just as well. However, the physical address and UPS/Fedex delivery options that such a service offers might be worth the extra charge.

Q: What size PO Box should I get?
A: Doesn't matter. Get the least expensive. If you get too much mail, or a large package, you'll be notified by the post office that you have a piece to pick up.

Q: What other options exist for getting a physical business address if I don't want to use my home address?
Try searching at google.com using the term "incubators" or "shared office space" Also check nbia.org (National Business Incubators Association)

Q: What monthly expenses can I expect running my business?
A: Everyone's business will be a little different. However, for a business such as the one I've described in this manual, here are some expenses you might encounter.

A sample of my own expenses:

VARIABLE EXPENSES (increase as sales increase)
Manufacturing/Printing/Duplicating $_____

ONE TIME FEES
Design (Website) $_____
Logo Design   *$ 25.00 (Gotlogos.com; no longer in biz)*
ISBN   *$225.00 (optional for book publishers)*

RECURRING MONTHLY
Paypal Merchant Fee   *$ 30.00/month*
Webhosting Fee $6.99/mo billed every 6 mos (1and1.com)
eFax $12.95
eVoice.com $ 4.95
Rent/Mortgage $250.00/month here on Saipan
Utilities $ 50.00/month here on Saipan
Bank Fees $ 0.00/month (no fee checking)
ATM Fees $_____
Cell phone/phone line $_____
Internet access $ 27.00/month here on Saipan
X-Payments $ 49.00/month (X-cart function

RECURRING ANNUALLY
SSL Certificate   *$49.00/year (1and1.com)*
Domain Registration $14.95/per domain (1and1.com) x 30
UPC Membership   *$_____ (Optionl for other manufacturer)*
PO Box rental in NYC   *$120.00/year United States PO Box*

OTHER EXPENSES
Travel $_____
Entertainment & Meals $_____
Misc Freelance $_____
Copying $_____
Advertising/Promotion $_____
Supplies $_____
Long Distance $_____
Ad in Magazine $_____
Subscriptions $_____
Miscellaneous $_____

DISCUSSION: Product

Q: Should I use Createspace's ISBN and UPC codes or my own?
A: It will be costlier for you to use your own as you'll have to purchase ISBN numbers directly ($175 for 1, or $275 for 10). It will be costlier to have your own UPC (Uniform Product Council) barcode because you'll have to pay an annual membership fee to be a UPC merchant (The fee is determined by the number of unique products a company needs to identify and as well as gross sales revenue).

However, that decision depends upon how much control you wish to have over your product and who people will need to contact in order to get copies. If Createspace™ assigns a UPC or ISBN, it means that THEY (not you) are listed as the publisher of that product throughout the industry. Thus, if a bookstore, wholesaler or library does a search for your product, they will contact Createspace™ for copies. That may result overall in more sales, but less control and direct contact with those distribution channels. You'll have to decide which is more important for you. I use my own ISBNs and UPC code for a few reasons that make my situation a little different. First, I'm a control freak. Second, I was a UPC merchant from back in 1990 when I had my record label, so I've been grandfathered into the system, and thus don't pay an annual fee. Third, I've been publishing books since 1992, so I already had a stash of ISBNs that I had paid for and could use to assign to all my books. Fourth, did I mention I'm a control freak? However, I do use Createspace's ISBN for <u>some</u> of my products (this manual for example).

DISCUSSION: Accepting Money

Q: What if I already have a merchant account?
A: No problem. You can continue to use the one you have. Or, if you see that you can get a better rate with the agent we suggest, and if you have the option to do so, you might consider changing.

Q: Will I be charged a fee even if I don't make sales?
A: Yes. Some companies will charge a "statement fee" as well as a "monthly minimum" (often $25-$40+) regardless of whether you make any sales or not. The company we suggest DOES NOT charge a minimum. If you use Paypal™ like I suggested, you will be charged $30/month.

Q: If I use a separate merchant processor other than Paypal™, what other fees can I expect to pay?
A: Some companies will charge:
Application fee- ($20 one-time avg)
Reprogramming- fee to set up your terminal ($200 one-time avg)
Statement fee- ($5-10/month)
Monthly minimum- ($20-$40+)
Terminal Leasing fee- ($varies)
Transaction fee- 1.5%-3.5% of amount charged

Q: If I use a different merchant processor other than Paypal™ should I lease my Transaction Capture machine and printer?
A: ABSOLUTELY NOT! There's no good reason to. I suggest that you purchase it outright.

Q: What if I live outside the US?
A: As of now, the Merchant Payments Pro option I recommend is available for US based individuals and companies. If you are not in the continental US, you will need to find a representative/processor in your area.

Q: How important is a good credit rating in getting approved?
A: According to our expert, of the top merchant companies Nova, PSI and Concord, each one in the list is more liberal and forgiving in their criteria for approving merchants. To lessen their risk, these companies will often place a limit on charge volume for first 3 months and then, as your history develops, they'll increase it. Paypal™, however, is a bit more lenient.

DISCUSSION: Web Presence

Q: Any tips for choosing a domain name?
A: You should choose a domain name that:
• reflects what your product does eg. If you're selling a product that helps people lose weight, for example, you may choose LoseWeight.com, WeightLossSecrets.com

• reflects how people know you or your product

• reflects how people may search for your product in a search engine

Also, avoid ambiguity or confusion. Choose words that everyone knows how to spell. Avoid words that may be misspelled, may confuse with i before e, may confuse If someone may ask is there an e at the end of this word? is that one "s" or two? is that "1" or the word "one"

Avoid using a "dot.net." If your ideal "dot.com" does not exist, choose something else. Tip: sometimes, names become available when the current owner fails to renew their ownership for the next year. If you are prepared to monitor it until it falls back into circulation, you might be able to secure your ideal name.

Avoid letters that may not be heard clearly is it "f" as in "frank" or "s" as in "sam" did she say "d" as in "david" or "t" as in tom?

Here is an example of someone who decided to go from a boring fact/feature type domain name (essupplements.com) to more memorable benefit, emotional-type one (JoeMuscle.com)...Keep this sort of thinking in mind as you think about ways to improve your own attractiveness to the public..-Walt
Fwd: essupplements is now JoeMuscle.com

A search at your favorite search engine using terms such as "choosing a domain name", "how to choose a domain" etc, should reveal some good results of articles with tips.

Q: What if I already have a domain name?
A: That's GREAT! You can always have more than one domain name "pointing" to the same site. For example, both my www.hiphopentrepreneur.com, and my www.hiphopbiz.com domain names take you to the same site. Having different domain names allows you to experiment to discover which one is easier for people to remember and which one may lend itself to unique marketing ideas.

Q: If I have more than one domain, should I have multiple pages?
A: That's not necessary, based on the answer to the previous question. However, if each page has a different content and different key word meta tags, it might prove helpful in securing multiple placement in search engines.

Q: What if someone owns the domain name I want?
A: Find another one. If you brainstorm long enough, you can come up with something that suits you perfectly. But, here's a tip: just because someone currently owns your desired domain name, doesn't mean you can't have it soon. If someone owns your domain name, but hasn't put up a site yet, they may not really have plans to.

Consequently, they may let their ownership lapse by not renewing their ownership with the registrar. When you check on the ownership using networksolutions.com's "WhoIs" Database, make note of the "record expires" date. It it's scheduled to expire in a few weeks or months, you might get lucky and be able to grab it if they don't renew. That's what happened to me: now I own HIPHOPBIZ.COM after the original owner failed to renew, AND, now someone else owns BOB-MARLEY.COM when I failed to renew back in 1997 when I reserved it. But, whatever you do, DO NOT, I repeat, DO NOT notify the current owner that you're interested in the domain name, unless you DESPERATELY, REALLY want it and are willing to pay them for it now that they know it now has value to you!

Q: Why should I use Powerpipe to reserve my domain name?
A: You don't have to, but currently, but while some companies charge $35US/year to own your domain name, Powerpipe™ charges about $10US.

Q: Okay, So, how do I register with PowerPipe.com?
A: Visit www.powerpipe.com
1. enter the desired domain name in search box
2. click on "go"
3. choose .com option if available and click to continue (red=not available, green=available)
4. choose 1 year option and "Free Parking"
5. click on "Add these names to my shopping cart"
6. shopping cart should read: 1 year registration ($10.10) with no hosting ($0)
7. click on Check out/Payment
8. enter your email address
9. To complete form:
a. choose master password
b. Enter your information as Domain Name Holder
c. choose Technical contact Same as Domain Holder:
d. here is the info you'll need for the host company info

HOSTNAME IP ADDRESS (example; important: you'll need the exact address of your particular hosting co. If you use 1and1 as I suggest, the info is

Primary Server: NS57.1AND1.COM
Secondary Server: NS58.1AND1.COM
10. click on submit
11. enter your credit card info
12. click on submit (you should receive a confirmation email)

Q: Will this manual help if I already have my business online?
A: YES. However, you will get more specific design information in my Websites That Sell Manual.

Q: Where can I learn more about HTML?
A: Try www.HTMLGoodies.com and do a search online for "html tutorial"

DISCUSSION: Promotion

Q: Should I purchase email names off the Internet?
A: ABSOLUTELY NOT. Unless it's an "opt-in" list where the names of the list belong to people who've specifically requested to be on the list. Otherwise, you'll make many enemies, and may even have your website shut down for sending unsolicited email. (a crime known as "spamming")

Q: What is MrConference.com?
A: FreeConferenceCall.com and MrConference are free teleconferencing services that allow you to have conference calls with up to 30 people. To have more people on the call will cost a little extra. Conference calls are good ways to interact with groups of your potential customers and clients.

Q: How can I get my site in the top 10 results in Google?
A: There's a whole branch of expertise known as Search Engine Optimization that shows you what to incorporate into your site design in order to help reach this goal. It helps if your site is linked to by many other sites. Pick up a copy of *Always on Top* by Kamau Austin, available at passionprofit.com/products.html

Q: How often should I communicate with my mailing list?
A: I find once per week to be an acceptable frequency. Once every two weeks may also be good. Unless you have a daily news like and entertainment column, or a horoscope feature that people want to read each day, you might be wise to keep it to no more than once per week.

DISCUSSION: Freedom

Q: When Do I quit my job?

A: I've recently been hosting a unique "Turn Your Passion Into INTERNET Profit" phone-in workshop. A limited number of participants are taken through an intensive, interactive course to help them get all the facts, guidance and step-by-step assistance to set up their business on the internet. During the last conference call, someone asked, "When do I quit my job?"

To have some fun with the answer, I replied, *"You quit your job when you want to be successful."* Other answers include *"You quit your job when you don't want to work there anymore!"* Or *"You quit your job when you want the alternative bad enough."*

My feeling is that most people would like to have a formula to use to determine when, at some time in the future, all the pieces of the puzzle are all in perfect alignment and they can cheerfully and confidently wave goodbye to their boss! The truth is, the answer to the question has nothing to do with any facts or figures and everything to do with your identity. When you are an entrepreneur in the deepest concept of yourself, you'll know the answer to "When do I quit my job?" For you see,

There's no such thing as future time
'cause time does not exist
to think there's more than now, dear friend's
a trap you must resist

It's tempting to construct your life
in terms of "if" and "when"
but "when" and "if" don't always show
and if they don't, what then?

Your question begs an answer
but assumes one lie is true
that somehow cause for what you'll do
exists outside of you

The critical decision
is not based on time or tide
whoever claims a formula
quite frankly, friend, they lied

You'll need to choose your view of you
despite what terms are met
and asking "when" might simply mean
you haven't chosen yet

Identity decides
the why and when of what we do
decide first who you are
and then you'll know what you should do

(For fish will do what fish will do
and that's the reason why
no pension, perk or paycheck
ever gets a fish to fly!)

Don't complicate the matter, then
with all this extra "stuff"
But simply choose by asking
"Do I want it bad enough?"

Walt's Life Rhyme #209
When Do I Quit?
Walt F.J. Goodridge
*"I share what I know,
so that others may grow!"*
Sign up for life rhymes at www.liferhymes.com

Q: When Do I quit my job? TAKE 2!

A: *And speaking of quitting a job (again), the following email was sent to me just two days ago, on Thursday, August 7. 2014. I've changed "S.R.'s" name for obvious reasons you'll discover! Enjoy and be inspired!*

"Walt,

thanks again for your coaching session back in June - it was very valuable and I'm going to go over the recording of it more carefully soon so as to make sure that I'm doing all of the things you suggested. Since our call, I've gone ahead and put up the website, created an LLC and am in the process of signing another artist. So things are moving in the right direction.

However, I must say that I got an amazing piece of news a couple days ago: I'm getting laid off! When I was busy hatching plans on how to get fired, something inside me told me to hang on a little longer, and sure enough, when I went to work this Monday morning, my boss immediately called me into a conference room, sat me down, and shook his head saying there was nothing he could do about it, my company is laying me off with the equivalent of 4-5-6 months of pay! Inside, I was jumping for joy, but I wanted to keep a calm, professional external demeanor that hid my joyous emotions, as that may be a bit awkward. Instead, I'll go through the motions and pretend like it's a tough time (they've already given me my final two weeks - that I was supposed to be working - off as a result).

Suffice to say, this is an amazing state of affairs and I couldn't be more excited. I'm rereading your book, Ducks in a Row now as it has new meaning now that I've parted ways with my desk job.

Anyways, just wanted to drop the good news. I'll probably be ready for another coaching session before too long but wanted to make sure you were aware of these developments. Thanks again for all your help thus far, Walt.

Sincerely,
S.R."

I REPLIED:
 hey, SR! Wow! That IS great! Yep, from my experience, that's how the universe works! Once you set an intention, the universe bends over backwards to bring it into fruition, despite how it may seem at first, and despite how it may seem to others!
 Keep riding the wave!
W

DISCUSSION: Final Words

Q: What if I have more questions?
A: Consider a single coaching session

Send an email to coaching@passionprofit.com to receive a coaching questionnaire and instructions on how to sign up for a single coaching session. In my opinion and practice, coaching shouldn't be a long-term commitment that depletes your income before you have a chance to make money! You complete a preliminary questionnaire, decide what you wish to accomplish, I decide if we can work together, and we schedule a single hour+ session that we record so you can return and refer to it in the future as you complete all the tasks that we outline.

You can always schedule future sessions, but the motivation to keep moving forward doesn't come from me. You must be a self-starter. Heck! As a nomadpreneur, I've got my own freedom to enjoy, I can't spend all my time coaching others! When would I have time to enjoy my own freedom???

Q: How may I contact you?
A: You may contact me at: walt@passionprofit.com

APPENDIX

Article: The Case for Createspace™
Article: The Power of the Penny
Glossary
Suggested Products from the Series
Free ebooks and ongoing support
Other books by Walt on different topics
About the Author

*****

SAMPLE PRESS RELEASE #1

"This is the actual press release I use each year for freesummerconcerts.com."

FOR IMMEDIATE RELEASE:

FREESUMMERCONCERTS.COM Announces 10th Year & 2014 Season of free concerts NATIONWIDE!
Once only for New Yorkers, free service now launches nationwide!

MAY 2014--Every summer, the nation's parks, piers, plazas and pathways host some of best musical entertainment in the world free to the public! From Rock, Jazz, Classical, R&B, Hip Hop, Country, Salsa and Reggae to Folk– an free, 8-year old online service helps residents and tourists stay on top of it all.

"Like many people, I was always hearing about free concerts I missed...usually a day later when everyone was talking about how much fun they had!" Goodridge explains, recounting how, in 2005, the idea for the site came to him. "So, one summer, I took the time to compile every event that was available here in New York, created a little computer program to email myself and a few friends reminders of what was happening each week. Word spread, and the rest, as they say, is history!"

The site, now enjoying its 10th summer season as the leading summer event aggregator in New York City, now boasts a calendar of over 1,600 events including Summerstage, Celebrate Brooklyn and the perennial Wingate Field and Seaside Concert series. It survives on a contribution strategy of contributions from a mailing list of loyal fans and followers–many of whom have been on board since the beginning.

Using that simple business model, Goodridge hopes to expand the service nationwide by employing a team of music mavens to franchise the concept for major metropolitan regions in each state!

Summer officially starts on June 21, but the FreeSummerConcerts fan base starts buzzing as early as January each year," Goodridge adds.

Learn more and Sign up at www.FreeSummerConcerts.com

###

Article: The Case for Createspace™

In a previous article "The Case for Self-Publishing, Walt's Way" I made the case that it can be and often is more profitable to be a self-published, print-on-demand author/publisher than to be signed to a major publishing house.

Well, the game just a got a whole lot easier, and that game can be played by sellers of music and videos, too! Whether you are an individual, business, church, school or business, what I'm about to share with you can help you easily and cost-effectively manufacture and sell your book, audio CD or video at a fraction of the cost, and a multiple of the profit of other options.

As the self-published author of 16 books, I always have my eyes open for better, faster and more cost-effective strategies for maximizing profits on book sales. So, when a friend recommended I take a look at Createspace™, a relatively new option for print-on-demand publishing and fulfillment for books, audio CDs and videos, I was open, even though I was happy with my then current printer.

Createspace™ is a print-on-demand (short-run) printer purchased by Amazon in 2007. Here are some of the benefits I discovered:

 Higher profits on Amazon sales compared to Advantage Program.

The main reason I got excited about Createspace was that I saw it would boost profits on my sales through the Amazon.com site. Let me explain.

Since Amazon.com is where an ever-increasing number of people go to purchase books, CDs and videos, the independent writer/artist needs to have a presence on that site. However, as many of us independent publishers know, sales of a single copy of our book through Amazon's Advantage® program is often a "loss leader." In other words, many of us agree to lose money on single copy sales, hoping that orders will increase with the popularity of the book. Let me give you an example. (These are actual numbers)

Let's say your book sells for $14.95 retail. When Amazon orders a single copy of your book for their inventory, they--like most wholesalers-will pay you 45 percent of the retail, that's $6.73. Now, the printing cost for your $14.95 book (let's assume a page count of 200 pages) might be about $3.85. Some printers may charge an additional per-book "set-up" charge of, say, $1.50 and shipping charge of about $3.79. Therefore, the total cost to manufacture and ship your book to Amazon for them to sell to their customer is $9.14. In other words, you would spend $9.14 and earn only $6.73. In still other words, you lose $2.41!

In such a scenario, however, you break even if Amazon ordered two copies, and you would finally start to make a profit if they ordered three copies or more-and they would if you asked them to-but that profit would be very small.

Now, however, with Createspace™ doing the printing and automatic fulfillment for Amazon orders (remember, they are essentially now the same company), it's like having Amazon print and fulfill the book orders through their site. You can now make a per copy "royalty" of $5.77! (You can visit the site and crunch the numbers yourself) So, now, on an order of a single copy of your title, you can go from losing $2.41 to earning $5.77!

But, that's not all. There are other benefits as well.

☑   **No need to manually fulfill Amazon Advantage® orders:** With Createspace™ automatically fulfilling orders for Amazon sales, you can free up more of your time to focus on promoting your book, CD or video.

☑   **No more "Out of Stock" notices on your title:** With Createspace™ doing the fulfillment, your title is always "In Stock." Before, if there happened to be zero copies in Amazon's inventory, a customer might place an order (provided they didn't get turned off by seeing "out of stock" in the listing), Amazon would notify you, then you'd have to print and send the order to Amazon's warehouse, which would then send the order to the customer; Now, it all happens seamlessly without your involvement.

☑   **Lower shipping costs for you and your customers.** Being part of Amazon's distribution system, Createspace™ can offer lower shipping costs for you and your customers.

☑   **Zero ($0) proof cost for CDs.** As of this writing, you can upload the MP3 files and graphics for your CD, and have a proof (CD, jewel case, inserts and printing on the CD) sent to you in a few days at absolutely no charge! It's a special promotion the duration of which has not been specified.

☑   **Computing royalties/profits is a bit easier.** Some of my titles are co-authored. With CS, I can view the (royalty) from each sale and split that with my co-author rather than having to do all sorts of intricate computations that included manufacturing and shipping costs for various channels.

☑   **Lower set-up cost.** Technically, there is no set-up cost to register your title with Createspace. You can upload a title interior and cover (pdf files) and start earning a commission right away.

However, if you want to earn the greatest possible commission from your sales, there is a $39 upgrade charge. That's essentially a set-up charge by another name, but even so, it's still less than the $80 other companies charge.

☑   **Cheaper Proof Cost.**
It was costing me $30 to receive a proof of my title. With Createspace, I only pay the "at cost" printing cost of $3.85 plus $3.61 basic shipping (total $7.46) to receive my proof!

Once I started using Createspace™, I discovered other positives:

☑ **Richer color. Thicker feel:** It could simply be normal variations in printers, but the color of the CreateSpaceT edition of the books I've since printed is darker and richer than before. For the book printing, the paper being used is also a bit thicker. The CDs are beautifully printed, and professionally duplicated. Your customers will be happy.

☑ **Fast review process:** After submitting a title for publishing or duplication, the review process to approve the submission is amazingly fast! I often upload a PDF or mp3 file and get a response the same day!

☑ **Great Customer & Phone Support.** CreateSpace customer service is fantastic! Emails are thorough, on point and well written, and I've never been on hold to reach someone.

☑ **Seamless transition from Advantage®:** If you're on the Advantage® program, the transition to Createspace is fast and seamless.

☑ **Accurate delivery estimate.** The proofs (and by extension, customers' orders) show up exactly when and often before they predict.

DRAWBACKS & CRITIQUE

✗ **All your eggs in one basket.** Prior to Createspace, I used my print-on-demand company to fill orders to Amazon Advantage. I still have my own online presence through which I receive orders directly from my customers.

✗ No way to track the identities of my customers. Amazon Advantage provided no way to track my customers either. However, using Createspace's e-store instead of my own online presence would give Createspace control of two streams of income and two customer databases to which I would have no access.

Conclusion:

Since launching my business on the Web in 1997, I've noticed that when it comes to book purchases, many people are opting to go to Amazon, rather than order directly from my individual publisher sites. In fact, prospective customers will even visit my site, get the information they need, then order from Amazon.

So, if that's going to happen anyway, then it makes sense to maximize the profit from the Amazon sales channel, and have Amazon (through Createspace) print and deliver the orders their customers are purchasing.

Second, for self-published authors who don't have the resources to print thousands of copies of a book, CD or video, it makes sense to (essentially) have Amazon print and deliver the products your customers are ordering. When you receive an order, simply log in to your Createspace account, print the number of copies you wish, and instruct Createspace to print and send the exact number of books to you or your customers anywhere in the world.

Article: The Power of the Penny

A friend of mine recently started blogging and, in his first few days, earned 48 cents through pay-per-click ads. "Forty-eight cents???" you ask. Yes, forty-eight cents! But before you start laughing, answer this question:

Which would you rather have: a penny doubled each day for a month or $10,000? If you haven't already encountered this question before, you might be tempted to take the $10,000. After all, $10,000 is $10,000, and a penny is only a penny, right? Even if they suspect that doubling a penny each day might result in a huge number, most people might not intuitively realize just how much is really at stake. Well, the correct answer—provided you want the option that will make you richer—is to take the penny option. Here's what you will receive each day for 30 days if you do:

On Day 1 – You receive 1 cent
Day 2 - 2 cents
Day 3 - 4 cents
Day 4 - 8 cents
Day 5 - 16 cents
Day 6 - 32 cents
Day 7 - 64 cents
Day 8 - $1.28
Day 9 - $2.56
Day 10 - $5.12
Day 11 - $10.24
Day 12 - $20.48
Day 13 - $40.96
Day 14 - $81.92
Day 15 - $163.84
Day 16 - $327.68
Day 17 - $655.36
Day 18 - $1,310.72
Day 19 - $2,621.44
Day 20 - $5,242.88
Day 21 - $10,485.76
Day 22 - $20,971.52
Day 23 - $41,943.04
Day 24 - $83,886.08
Day 25 - $167,772.16
Day 26 - $335,544.32
Day 27 - $671,088.64
Day 28 - $1,342,177.28
Day 29 - $2,684,354.56
Day 30 - $5,368,709.12

Seen for what it is, this example is truly astounding! A single penny, doubled for an entire month yields a final day's payout of over 5 million dollars, AND a total accumulated payoff of over 10 million! It's an example of growth which progresses not arithmetically (i.e. by single units) but by what's known as "geometric progression. It's also called a geometric sequence or a geometric series-a sequence of numbers where each term after the first is found by multiplying the previous term by a fixed number called the "common ratio." Like the progression of rewards on the popular game show "Who Wants To Be A Millionaire," which starts at $100 and grows to a $1 million payoff in just 12 questions, by roughly doubling each prize (common ratio=2), the concept of geometric growth is indeed a powerful one.

But enough math. How does this apply to your business as a passionpreneur? Well, you can apply the principle of the doubling penny in your marketing and advertising to sell more products and grow your business.

However, before you get too excited, keep in mind that the reason many people never realize the full potential of their marketing and advertising efforts is simply this: They don't have the patience to see it through to the final payoff! Look back at our penny example for a moment, and notice how slowly the rewards seem to grow. A week after you've started, your daily take is still just 64 cents. Fifteen days later-fully half way through the process-your daily take is just $163, just 0.00305 percent of what it will be on the final day. (That's LESS than 1/2 of 1/10 of 1 percent!) Two-thirds of the way through at day 20, your payoff is $5242.88, just about 1/10 of a percent of what the reward will be on the final day. So for many people, unable to gauge how the momentum of a marketing campaign is really growing, abandon it before reaching the equivalent of their "Day 30" payoff.

Now imagine if the numbers in our penny example represented the number of people who bought your product. Or, let's be conservative, and say it represents the number of people who merely HEAR about your product. And let's say that only 1 percent of these people purchase your product for $25. That's 53,687 people x $25 = sales of $1,342,177.25.

Success in marketing is really a numbers game. The more people you tell, the more people become your customers. Do not be discouraged by what appears to be a small start and small rewards. Once you launch your business using the Quick Start Formula, then continued persistence in your day by day efforts will eventually pay off!

For the full article,"The Power of the Penny," visit
http://www.waltgoodridge.com/the-power-of-the-penny

Glossary

condition formula: one of a set of proven strategies one can take to move the state of a given situation, project, business, or relationship from one state to a higher state of survival. The formulas names include "Non Existence," "Danger," "Emergency," "Normal," "Affluence," Power Change," and "Power."

domain: Your web address (eg. www.passionprofit.com) is known as a domain, or domain name.

FTP: File Transfer Protocol is the process by which the files that make up your website are uploaded and saved onto your hosting companies servers so that they can be accessed by people on the internet. You can use a program like "Fetch" (for Macs) or WSFTP (for PCs) to "ftp" your files.

HTML: Hyper-text Markup Language is the code that constitutes your web page. Next time you visit a website, click on "View→view source code," or right click on a blank space on the page and find the "view source" option and you will see what raw HTML code looks like.

merchant account: Setting up a merchant account allows you to accept and process credit cards from your customers.

non-existence: The condition formula of most importance to a new business or individual starting a new position or job.

nomadpreneur: The condition formula of most importance to a new business or individual starting a new position or job

passion: a hobby, talent or interest.

passionpreneur: someone who has use a passion as the basis of an entrepreneurial venture.

product: a high quality object or service in the hands of a consumer in exchange for something of value. It is not a product if it has not been exchanged for value.

SSL: Secure Socket Layer is a way for computers, web browsers and servers to communicate that keeps information encrypted, private and secure.

APPENDIX: Suggested products in the PassionProfit™ Series
Collect the whole set! ☺

❏ *Turn Your Passion Into Profit™: A Step-by-Step Guide for Turning ANY Hobby, Talent, Interest or Product idea into a money-making venture!*
Discover the profit in your passion. Make money doing what you love!

Paperback: $24.95; Ebook: $16.95
ebook: http://www.passionprofit.com/store/product.php?productid=24

❏ *The Websites That Sell Manual*
There is an art and a science to designing a website that communicates your value, heightens your credibility, inspires consumer confidence and compels visitors to whip out their credit cards and order your product or service online! There are some things you should NEVER do, and other things you absolutely MUST if you want to make money online.

Paperback: $19.95; Ebook: $16.95
ebook: http://www.passionprofit.com/store/product.php?productid=25

❏ *Turn Your Passion Into Profit 6-CD Audio Set Now Available!*
Turn Your Passion into Profit is now available as an audio series. Listen to Walt explain the entire passion to profit philosophy and formula. These six audio CDS include live workshops, coaching sessions and more.

CD: $49.95
cd: http://www.passionprofit.com/store/product.php?productid=20

❑ *Living True to Your Self*

Living true to your self requires that you adopt a new belief system about what's true for yourself, about others, and about the world you live in. It requires that you identify your purpose, develop an effective survival strategy, overcome inertia, motivate your self consistently, sustain momentum, decipher life's code to recognize the opportunities and harness the power in the setbacks, evolve in the direction of life's clues, while honoring body, mind and spirit...and that's just for starters! Walt shows you how!

Paperback: $19.95 ; ebook: $16

ebook: http://www.passionprofit.com/store/product.php?productid=83

❑ *Ducks in a Row??? Please. How to find the courage to finally QUIT your soul-draining, life-sapping, energy-depleting, freedom-robbing job now...before it's too late..and live passionately ever after!* The "prequel" to *Turn Your Passion Into Profit*. It takes a special way of thinking to walk away from a "good job!"

Paperback: $9.95 ; ebook: $4.95

ebook: http://www.passionprofit.com/store/product.php?productid=87

❑ *Nomadpreneur SECRETS Report*

This is the answer to the question: "Walt, how are you able to travel the world without a job?" A special report available only when you purchase *Websites That Sell*! A wise business person wouldn't reveal ALL his trade secrets, but I reveal more than most because (a) I don't believe in or fear competition, (b) I live true to my life's mission to "share what I know so that others may grow!"

Order Websites That Sell

ebook: http://www.passionprofit.com/store/product.php?productid=25

❏ *The Tao of Wow & The Art of Wow*

Find your wow factor! Make the world go wow!

Paperback only: $16.95;
http://www.passionprofit.com/store/product.php?productid=22

You are reading this title:

☑ The "Quick Start" Manual

I've launched business ventures and made sales in as little as 48 hours! Now you can achieve the same results by using this convenient step-by-step, action checklist! I'll share the methods, as well as the specific vendors, sites and software I use to get my own and my clients' operations up and running from idea to income as quickly as possible! Perhaps you'll beat my quick start record!

Paperback: $19.95 ; ebook: $16.00
http://www.passionprofit.com/store/product.php?productid=18

All titles and more are available at www.passionprofit.com/store

APPENDIX: FREE EBOOKS AND ONGOING SUPPORT

"Join my PassionProfit mailing list at http://www.passionprofit.com/free and receive the following ebooks free of charge, and receive weekly information, inspiration and ideas to help you turn your passion into profit!"

5. ❑ Get these FREE ebooks! ❑

All available free by joining the Turn Your Passion Into Profit™ mailing list at http://www.passionprofit.com/free

In Search of a Better Belief System

7 Conversations to Freedom

How to Become a Nomadpreneur

5. ❑ Find me online ❑

See all of my books at www.waltgoodridge.com/books

5. ❑ Read me online ❑

See an archive of (most of) my articles at www.saipanpreneur.com/archives

5. ❑ Follow me online ❑

Facebook: http://www.facebook.com/passionprophet

Twitter: @whereiswalt

Nomad Blog: www.jamaicaninchina.com

APPENDIX: Other books by Walt on different topics

❏ Health and Ageless Living ❏

The Ageless Adept
Yesterday's You
Fit to Breed
Fast & Grow Young

❏ Saipan ❏

Jamaican on Saipan
Saipan Living
Doing Business on Saipan
Chicken Feathers & Garlic Skin
From Bugle Boy to Battleship

❏ Hip Hop Entrepreneuring ❏

Change the Game
This Game of Hip Hop Artist Management
Hip Hop Record Label Business Plan

❏ Travel & Nomadpreneuring ❏

Jamaican in China (aka "Guess Who's Coming to Dim Sum")
The Coffeepot Cookbook

❏ Relationships ❏

If you want to be my girlfriend

View all at http://www.waltgoodridge.com/books

APPENDIX: About The Author

"Once upon a time, there was a Jamaican civil engineer who hated his job, followed his passion, started a sideline business, quit his job, ran off to a tropical island in the Pacific, and started a tourism business so he could give tours of the island to pretty girls every day and live a nomadpreneur's dream life!"

The author on Saipan, Northern Mariana Islands

A Columbia University graduate with a Bachelor of Science degree in civil engineering, Walt was, like many people, destined for a career in his profession of training. In fact, immediately after graduating, he accepted a job working in the Design Division of the Port Authority Engineering department on the 73rd floor of World Trade Center One. However, within the first fifteen minutes of this his first job in corporate America, Walt, frustrated by the monotony, restrictions of nine-to-five employment, realized beyond the shadow of a doubt, that he absolutely hated it!

It was several years until he was able to grow his sideline business in the music industry--a personal passion--and walk away from his career to become a full-time "passionpreneur." He authored several books on the music industry, created a brand of inspiration called "Life Rhymes," and launched dozens of websites, and unique products.

As he honed his experience and expertise in website development, internet marketing, and living true to himself, he developed a unique "Passion Profit Philosophy and Formula" and a coaching practice to help others do the same. In 1999, he published the formula in *Turn Your Passion into Profit* which, with yearly updates, has consistently sold in the top 50 in home-business books on Amazon.com.

A few years later Walt booked a one-way ticket, escaped the rat race to live out his dream of being a "nomadpreneur."

Walt currently owns and operates over 50 websites, has written more than 30 books, over 400 articles and over 500 motivational poems. He has been an artist manager, radio deejay, record label owner, inventor, poet, network marketer and consultant. He has written for Entrepreneur Magazine and Black Enterprise, and has been featured in Time Magazine, Wall Street Journal Online, the Dallas Morning News, The Kip Business Report and numerous publications and websites.

Walt is originally from the island of Jamaica, and now lives a vegan lifestyle on the island of Saipan. You may contact Walt at P.O. Box 618 Church Street Station, New York NY 10008 or calling (646) 481-4238 or via email at Walt@passionprofit.com.

www.ingramcontent.com/pod-product-compliance
Lightning Source LLC
Chambersburg PA
CBHW081303170526
45165CB00011B/3395

* 9 7 8 1 4 5 1 5 4 5 7 0 8 *

www.ingramcontent.com/pod-product-compliance
Lightning Source LLC
Chambersburg PA
CBHW081303170526
45165CB00011B/3395